CAMBRIDGE LINCOL

Shakespeare

King Henry IV

Part 1

Edited by Rex Gibson

Series Editor: Rex Gibson
Director, Shakespeare and Schools Project

CAMBRIDGE
UNIVERSITY PRESS

PUBLISHED BY THE PRESS SYNDICATE OF THE UNIVERSITY OF CAMBRIDGE
The Pitt Building, Trumpington Street, Cambridge CB2 1RP, United Kingdom

CAMBRIDGE UNIVERSITY PRESS
The Edinburgh Building, Cambridge CB2 2RU, United Kingdom
40 West 20th Street, New York, NY 10011–4211, USA
10 Stamford Road, Oakleigh, Melbourne 3166, Australia

First published 1998

Printed in the United Kingdom at J. W. Arrowsmith Limited, Bristol

Typeset in Ehrhardt

A catalogue record for this book is available from the British Library

Library of Congress Cataloguing in Publication data applied for

ISBN 0 521 62689 7

Prepared for publication by Stenton Associates
Designed by Richard Morris, Stonesfield Design
Picture research by Callie Kendall

Thanks are due to the following for permission to reproduce photographs:

Cover, © Donald Cooper/Photostage; 16, 116, 125 191*tl*, © Donald Cooper/Photostage;
39, Shakespeare Centre Library, Stratford-upon-Avon; 68, Solihull News/photo:
Shakespeare Centre Library, Stratford-upon-Avon; 87; Laurence Burns; 100, Joe Cocks
Studio Collection/Shakespeare Centre Library; 142, 176, Nobby Clark; 151, 191*b*, Richard
Mildenhall/Arena; 191*tr*, Angus McBean/Shakespeare Centre Library; 193 Hulton Getty
Collection; 203, M. Franck/Magnum

Contents

Cambridge School Shakespeare

This edition of *Henry IV Part 1* is part of the *Cambridge School Shakespeare* series. Like every other play in the series, it has been specially prepared to help all students in schools and colleges.

This *Henry IV Part 1* aims to be different from other editions of the play. It invites you to bring the play to life in your classroom, hall or drama studio through enjoyable activities that will increase your understanding. Actors have created their different interpretations of the play over the centuries. Similarly, you are encouraged to make up your own mind about *Henry IV Part 1*, rather than having someone else's interpretation handed down to you.

Cambridge School Shakespeare does not offer you a cut-down or simplified version of the play. This is Shakespeare's language, filled with imaginative possibilities. You will find on every left-hand page: a summary of the action, an explanation of unfamiliar words, and a choice of activities on Shakespeare's language, characters and stories.

Between each act and in the pages at the end of the play, you will find notes, illustrations and activities. These will help to increase your understanding of the whole play.

There are a large number of activities to give you the widest choice to suit your own particular needs. Please don't think you have to do every one. Choose the activities that help you most.

This edition will be of value to you whether you are studying for an examination, reading for pleasure, or thinking of putting on the play to entertain others. You can work on the activities on your own or in groups. Many of the activities suggest a particular group size, but don't be afraid to make up smaller or larger groups to suit your own purposes.

Although you are invited to treat *Henry IV Part 1* as a play, you don't need special dramatic or theatrical skills to do the activities. By choosing your activities, and by exploring and experimenting, you can make your own interpretations of Shakespeare's language, characters and stories. Whatever you do, remember that Shakespeare wrote his plays to be acted, watched and enjoyed.

Rex Gibson

This edition of *Henry IV Part 1* uses the text of the play established by Herbert Weil and Judith Weil in *The New Cambridge Shakespeare*.

Before the play begins

Shakespeare's play dramatises the power struggles in early fifteenth-century England caused by Henry IV's dubious claim to be the rightful king. Henry had forced King Richard II from the throne in 1399 and was probably responsible for Richard's murder shortly afterwards. But as this family tree shows, Henry's claim was weak. By the custom of male primogeniture (inheritance through the older son), the descendants of Lionel had a stronger claim than those of John of Gaunt:

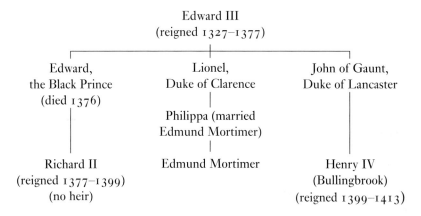

Edward III
(reigned 1327–1377)

| Edward, the Black Prince (died 1376) | Lionel, Duke of Clarence | John of Gaunt, Duke of Lancaster |

Philippa (married Edmund Mortimer)

| Richard II (reigned 1377–1399) (no heir) | Edmund Mortimer | Henry IV (Bullingbrook) (reigned 1399–1413) |

Shakespeare's play *Richard II* portrays the events that brought Henry to the throne. King Richard banished Henry (Bullingbrook) and confiscated his land and titles. Henry returned from exile, deposed Richard and had himself crowned king.

Henry did not enjoy peaceful possession of the crown. He was beset by attacks from Wales and Scotland and challenged by his former allies the Percy family, who supported Edmund Mortimer's claim to be rightful king of England. As the play opens, Henry, wearied by warfare, and seeking to appease his troubled conscience by leading a crusade to the Holy Land, expresses his anxiety and exhaustion:

'So shaken as we are, so wan with care'

But Shakespeare did far more than portray the military and political events of the unquiet times of Henry IV. His dramatic imagination created the character who would ensure the play's lasting success from the moment of its first performance: Falstaff.

The world of the play

List of characters

The Court

KING HENRY IV
PRINCE HAL   his eldest son, Prince of Wales
PRINCE JOHN OF LANCASTER   his third son

Earl of WESTMORELAND
SIR WALTER BLUNT

The Rebels

Earl of NORTHUMBERLAND   (Lord Percy)
HOTSPUR   his son (Harry Percy)
Earl of WORCESTER   Northumberland's brother
LADY PERCY   Hotspur's wife

OWEN GLENDOWER   a Welsh Prince
MORTIMER   claimant to the crown
LADY MORTIMER   Glendower's daughter
SIR MICHAEL DOUGLAS   a Scottish warlord

SIR RICHARD VERNON
ARCHBISHOP OF YORK

The Tavern

SIR JOHN FALSTAFF
BARDOLPH   Falstaff's follower
POINS   Prince Hal's friend
PETO   Prince Hal's follower

HOSTESS
VINTNER
FRANCIS   a drawer
    (barman)

The Robbery at Gad's Hill

GADSHILL   a highwayman
FIRST CARRIER
SECOND CARRIER
OSTLER   a stableman

CHAMBERLAIN
FIRST TRAVELLER
SECOND TRAVELLER
SHERIFF

Servants, messengers, soldiers, travellers, attendants

The action of the play takes place at various locations
in England and Wales.

King Henry, weary and pale, seeks to end civil war in which Englishmen fight Englishmen. He proposes a Crusade to the Holy Land to seize Jerusalem from non-Christians.

1 King Henry: first impressions (in pairs)

Explore ways of speaking Henry's lines 1–33 to find what kind of man you think he is. For example, is he strong and determined, or weak and unsure, worn out with civil war and the affairs of state? One clue might be in how he speaks the four repetitions of 'No more' in lines 5, 7, 15 and 18.

2 Imagery

Henry uses vivid imagery to describe an England torn by civil war. Suggest what pictures are conjured up in your mind by the images of peace (line 2), England (lines 5–6), war (lines 7–9), rival armies in a civil war (lines 9–13) and peace (lines 14–18).

3 A Crusade: Henry's mixed motives

In medieval times, many Englishmen went on Crusades to the distant shores of the Holy Land ('strands afar remote') in the belief that helping to recapture Jerusalem ('the sepulchre of Christ') for Christianity would gain pardon for their sins. Lines 24–7 describe graphically how the Crusaders thought of their task: to regain the land where Jesus was crucified to redeem humanity ('For our advantage').

King Henry may wish to atone for having had King Richard II killed and seizing his throne (see page 1). Another motive might be to unite his quarrelling nobles against a common enemy. As you work through the play, keep in mind that Henry is a man with a troubled conscience and a host of political problems.

wan pale	**close** hand to hand fighting
broils quarrels, wars	**impressèd** conscripted
flow'rets tiny flowers	**levy** recruit
one nature ... bred the same family	**arms** weapons of war
intestine shock internal battle	**bootless** useless

King Henry IV Part 1

ACT 1   SCENE 1
London: King Henry's palace

Enter the KING, LORD JOHN OF LANCASTER, EARL OF WESTMORELAND,
SIR WALTER BLUNT, with others

KING So shaken as we are, so wan with care,
  Find we a time for frighted peace to pant,
  And breathe short-winded accents of new broils
  To be commenced in strands afar remote;
  No more the thirsty entrance of this soil   5
  Shall daub her lips with her own children's blood,
  No more shall trenching war channel her fields
  Nor bruise her flow'rets with the armèd hoofs
  Of hostile paces. Those opposèd eyes
  Which, like the meteors of a troubled heaven,   10
  All of one nature, of one substance bred,
  Did lately meet in the intestine shock
  And furious close of civil butchery,
  Shall now in mutual well-beseeming ranks
  March all one way, and be no more opposed   15
  Against acquaintance, kindred, and allies.
  The edge of war, like an ill-sheathèd knife,
  No more shall cut his master. Therefore, friends,
  As far as to the sepulchre of Christ –
  Whose soldier now, under whose blessèd cross 20
  We are impressèd and engaged to fight –
  Forthwith a power of English shall we levy,
  Whose arms were moulded in their mother's womb
  To chase these pagans in those holy fields
  Over whose acres walked those blessèd feet   25
  Which fourteen hundred years ago were nailed
  For our advantage on the bitter cross.
  But this our purpose now is twelve month old,
  And bootless 'tis to tell you we will go.

Westmoreland reports that bad news from Wales and the North interrupted the planning of the Crusade. Henry says that he has just been told of the defeat of the Scots by Hotspur.

1 News! (in groups of seven or more)

Henry's plans for a Crusade to the Holy Land are disrupted by news of attacks by the Welsh and the Scots. In Wales an English army has been defeated. Its commander, Mortimer, has been taken prisoner and the English dead have been savagely mutilated. At a bloody battle at Holmedon near the border with Scotland, the English under Hotspur have defeated ('discomfited') a Scottish army led by the Earl of Douglas. The battle was fought on 'Holy-rood day' (Holy Cross day): 14 September 1403.

The news arrived at Henry's court at different times and by different messengers. Take the following roles and prepare a sequence for performance:

King Henry's Council (three or more students): Your task is to plan the Crusade proposed by the king (lines 34–5), and to question the messengers.

Messenger from Wales: You report the terrible fate of the English forces led by Mortimer (lines 36–46).

Messenger from Holmedon: You report the battle (lines 50–61), and you may be asked to explain why you left when the fighting was at its height ('pride of their contention').

Sir Walter Blunt: Your task is to report to the king the outcome of the battle of Holmedon (lines 62–73).

King Henry: You receive Sir Walter's news, and make sure that he gives you full details. But your mind may also be full of the Crusade you plan, so begin your preparation by speaking lines 47–8 in different ways.

---

forwarding ... expedience
  planning the Crusade
hot ... charge set down hotly
  discussed, and officers' duties
  planned
all athwart upsetting our plans

post messenger
tidings news
Archibald Earl of Douglas
shape of likelihood probable result
new lighted recently dismounted
seat of ours palace

Therefor we meet not now. Then let me hear 30
Of you, my gentle cousin Westmoreland,
What yesternight our Council did decree
In forwarding this dear expedience.

WESTMORELAND My liege, this haste was hot in question,
And many limits of the charge set down 35
But yesternight, when all athwart there came
A post from Wales, loaden with heavy news,
Whose worst was that the noble Mortimer,
Leading the men of Herefordshire to fight
Against the irregular and wild Glendower, 40
Was by the rude hands of that Welshman taken,
A thousand of his people butcherèd,
Upon whose dead corpse there was such misuse,
Such beastly shameless transformation,
By those Welshwomen done, as may not be 45
Without much shame retold or spoken of.

KING It seems then that the tidings of this broil
Brake off our business for the Holy Land.

WESTMORELAND This, matched with other, did, my gracious lord,
For more uneven and unwelcome news 50
Came from the north, and thus it did import:
On Holy-rood day, the gallant Hotspur there,
Young Harry Percy, and brave Archibald,
That ever valiant and approvèd Scot,
At Holmedon met, where they did spend 55
A sad and bloody hour;
As by discharge of their artillery,
And shape of likelihood, the news was told;
For he that brought them, in the very heat
And pride of their contention did take horse, 60
Uncertain of the issue any way.

KING Here is a dear and true industrious friend,
Sir Walter Blunt, new lighted from his horse,
Stained with the variation of each soil
Betwixt that Holmedon and this seat of ours; 65
And he hath brought us smooth and welcome news.
The Earl of Douglas is discomfited.
Ten thousand bold Scots, two-and-twenty knights,

King Henry gives details of Hotspur's magnificent victory and regrets
that his own son Hal does not possess Hotspur's honourable qualities.
Henry is enraged by Hotspur's refusal to give up his prisoners.

1 Who's who? (in pairs)

Henry or Westmoreland provide descriptions of most of the major
characters who appear in the political plot of the play. Write down two
or three words used to describe each of the following: Hotspur, Hal,
Worcester, Glendower, Mortimer, Douglas, Sir Walter Blunt. Using
your descriptions, take turns to strike a pose as one of the characters.
Your partner guesses which character you portray.

2 Hotspur and Hal, contrasting sons

King Henry's lines 77–89 are the first mention of a contrast that will
run through the play, Hotspur versus Hal. Hotspur is 'the theme of
honour's tongue' (always praised by honour), but Hal is stained by 'riot
and dishonour'. Henry is so disappointed with his own son that he calls
on an ancient belief that fairies stole healthy babies and left sickly ones
in their place. He wishes it could be proved that 'some night-tripping
fairy' had exchanged Hal for Hotspur in their cradles.

   As you read on, keep thinking about how far you agree with Henry's
assessment of his own son, Hal, in contrast with Northumberland's
son, Hotspur.

3 Prisoners of war

It was customary for a victor in battle to keep all his prisoners and to
profit from the ransom money paid. Only prisoners of royal blood had
to be handed over to the king. According to the rules of war of the time,
Hotspur seems to be acting legally. Suggest two or three reasons why
Henry is so angered by Hotspur's refusal to give up his prisoners.

Balked piled up like ridges left by
   a plough
spoil plunder from battle
blest blessed
grove wood
minion favourite, darling

Plantagenet (family name of the
   Royal family)
prune preen (like a hawk preening
   its feathers)
bristle up/The crest arouse the
   fighting spirit
holy purpose Crusade

Balked in their own blood, did Sir Walter see
On Holmedon's plains. Of prisoners Hotspur took   70
Mordake, Earl of Fife and eldest son
To beaten Douglas, and the Earl of Atholl,
Of Murray, Angus, and Menteith.
And is not this an honourable spoil?
A gallant prize? Ha, cousin, is it not?   75
WESTMORELAND In faith, it is a conquest for a prince to boast of.
KING Yea, there thou makest me sad, and makest me sin
In envy that my Lord Northumberland
Should be the father to so blest a son –
A son who is the theme of honour's tongue,   80
Amongst a grove the very straightest plant,
Who is sweet Fortune's minion and her pride –
Whilst I by looking on the praise of him
See riot and dishonour stain the brow
Of my young Harry. O that it could be proved   85
That some night-tripping fairy had exchanged
In cradle-clothes our children where they lay,
And called mine Percy, his Plantagenet!
Then would I have his Harry, and he mine.
But let him from my thoughts. What think you, coz,   90
Of this young Percy's pride? The prisoners
Which he in this adventure hath surprised
To his own use he keeps, and sends me word
I shall have none but Mordake, Earl of Fife.
WESTMORELAND This is his uncle's teaching, this is Worcester, 95
Malevolent to you in all aspects,
Which makes him prune himself, and bristle up
The crest of youth against your dignity.
KING But I have sent for him to answer this;
And for this cause a while we must neglect   100
Our holy purpose to Jerusalem.
Cousin, on Wednesday next our Council we
Will hold at Windsor, so inform the lords.
But come yourself with speed to us again,
For more is to be said and to be done   105
Than out of anger can be utterèd.
WESTMORELAND I will, my liege.   *Exeunt*

Prince Hal says that Falstaff is interested only in drinking, eating and fornicating. Falstaff claims that he and fellow thieves are governed by the moon. Hal warns that such men end on the gallows.

1 Contrasting scenes (in small groups)

Scene 2 sharply contrasts with Scene 1. From anxious discussion of political affairs, the atmosphere changes to one of joking about thievery, and the pleasures of eating, drinking and sex. To signify the shift from a serious to a comic world, Shakespeare moves from verse to prose.

Work out how to stage the opening of Scene 2 to bring out the contrast.

2 Fencing with language (in pairs)

Hal and Falstaff joke together like sword-fencers or jousting knights, each trying to get the advantage of the other. They constantly seize on each other's language, giving it a new twist in their replies. When Falstaff asks the time of day, Hal accuses him of having no real interest in time, because he lives only for the immediate pleasures of the body. Falstaff agrees, saying he belongs to the night, not the day, and like the sea, is ruled by the moon. Hal develops the moon image, comparing the flow and ebb of the sea to the life and death of thieves.

To gain a first impression of the two men, take parts and speak lines 1–85. Don't pause to work out words or phrases you don't understand. When you have time, the explanations below and at the foot of each page can help you. Remember that explaining puns can kill humour stone dead!

'grace' (line 13) – lordship, or nobleness, or blessing before a meal

'roundly' (line 18) – tell it truthfully, or Falstaff's belly

'steal' (line 24) – rob, or creep

'Lay by!' (line 29) – Stand and deliver!

'Bring in' (line 30) – More drink!

---

sack Spanish white wine
capons roast chickens
bawds prostitutes
dials clock faces
leaping-houses brothels
superfluous over-inquisitive
Phoebus (in Greek mythology) the sun god

troth true promise
Marry By the Virgin Mary (a mild oath)
squires personal attendants
Diana (in Roman mythology) goddess of the moon and chastity
countenance face, patronage

ACT 1 SCENE 2
London: a room in the palace

Enter PRINCE OF WALES and SIR JOHN FALSTAFF

FALSTAFF Now Hal, what time of day is it, lad?

PRINCE Thou art so fat-witted with drinking of old sack, and unbuttoning thee after supper, and sleeping upon benches after noon, that thou hast forgotten to demand that truly which thou wouldst truly know. What a devil hast thou to do with the time of the day? Unless hours were cups of sack, and minutes capons, and clocks the tongues of bawds, and dials the signs of leaping-houses, and the blessed sun himself a fair hot wench in flame-coloured taffeta, I see no reason why thou shouldst be so superfluous to demand the time of the day. 5

FALSTAFF Indeed, you come near me now, Hal, for we that take purses go by the moon and the seven stars, and not 'by Phoebus, he, that wandering knight so fair'. And I prithee, sweet wag, when thou art king, as God save thy grace – majesty, I should say, for grace thou wilt have none – 10

PRINCE What, none? 15

FALSTAFF No, by my troth, not so much as will serve to be prologue to an egg and butter.

PRINCE Well, how then? Come, roundly, roundly.

FALSTAFF Marry then, sweet wag, when thou art king let not us that are squires of the night's body be called thieves of the day's beauty. Let us be Diana's foresters, gentlemen of the shade, minions of the moon. And let men say we be men of good government, being governed as the sea is, by our noble and chaste mistress the moon, under whose countenance we steal. 20

PRINCE Thou sayest well, and it holds well too, for the fortune of us that are the moon's men doth ebb and flow like the sea, being governed as the sea is, by the moon. As for proof now: a purse of gold most resolutely snatched on Monday night, and most dissolutely spent on Tuesday morning, got with swearing 'Lay by!', and spent with crying 'Bring in!', now in as low an ebb as the foot of the ladder, and by and by in as high a flow as the ridge of the gallows. 25

Hal and Falstaff continue their joking. Beneath Hal's humour are reminders of imprisonment, hangings and poverty. Falstaff, in the style of a Puritan preacher, tells of criticism of Hal's conduct.

1 What's the joke? (in groups of three)

Much of the wordplay between Hal and Falstaff depends on knowledge that was familiar to Elizabethan audiences, but is now obscure. Today, actors help audiences to understand through physical and facial expressions and by the tone, emphasis and style of how they speak.

Take parts as a director and two actors. The director explains the following notes to the actors, adding practical suggestions for delivery on stage. The two actors ask questions and make their own suggestions:

line 35 'buff jerkin' – constable's leather jacket. Is Hal implying that Falstaff will be arrested?

lines 45–6 'here apparent', 'heir apparent'. Both could be pronounced 'hare' in Shakespeare's time. Is Falstaff making a terrible pun to make Hal and the audience groan?

lines 56–7 'suits'. Another pun: petitions, or a reference to hangmen being entitled to keep the clothes of the persons they executed.

lines 58–62 Six or seven similes for melancholy ('gib cat' = a howling tomcat; 'lugged' = cruelly tormented; 'Lincolnshire bagpipe' = windbag?). How can we help the audience here?

line 62 'Moorditch' – a foul-smelling open ditch in London where beggars gathered. Is Hal needling Falstaff about what might happen to him?

lines 64–9 The style is that of a Puritan preacher of the time calling on people to repent ('commodity of good names' = supply of decent reputations; 'rated' = criticised).

Hybla town in Sicily, famous for honey
old lad of the castle see page 193
durance imprisonment
quips, quiddities jokes, quibbles
reckoning payment for sex or drink

resolution thus fubbed enterprise robbed of its reward
rusty curb restraint
Father Antic buffoon, fool
jumps with my humour fits my personality

FALSTAFF By the Lord thou sayest true, lad – and is not my Hostess of
the tavern a most sweet wench?

PRINCE As the honey of Hybla, my old lad of the castle.
And is not a buff jerkin a most sweet robe of durance?   35

FALSTAFF How now, how now, mad wag? What, in thy quips and thy
quiddities? What a plague have I to do with a buff jerkin?

PRINCE Why, what a pox have I to do with my Hostess of the tavern?

FALSTAFF Well, thou hast called her to a reckoning many a time and
oft.   40

PRINCE Did I ever call for thee to pay thy part?

FALSTAFF No, I'll give thee thy due, thou hast paid all there.

PRINCE Yea, and elsewhere, so far as my coin would stretch, and
where it would not, I have used my credit.

FALSTAFF Yea, and so used it that were it not here apparent that thou   45
art heir apparent – but I prithee, sweet wag, shall there be gallows
standing in England when thou art king? And resolution thus
fubbed as it is with the rusty curb of old Father Antic the law? Do
not thou when thou art king hang a thief.

PRINCE No, thou shalt.   50

FALSTAFF Shall I? O rare! By the Lord, I'll be a brave judge!

PRINCE Thou judgest false already! I mean thou shalt have the hanging
of the thieves, and so become a rare hangman.

FALSTAFF Well, Hal, well! And in some sort it jumps with my humour
– as well as waiting in the court, I can tell you.   55

PRINCE For obtaining of suits?

FALSTAFF Yea, for obtaining of suits, whereof the hangman hath no
lean wardrobe. 'Sblood, I am as melancholy as a gib cat, or a lugged
bear.

PRINCE Or an old lion, or a lover's lute.   60

FALSTAFF Yea, or the drone of a Lincolnshire bagpipe.

PRINCE What sayest thou to a hare, or the melancholy of Moorditch?

FALSTAFF Thou hast the most unsavoury similes, and art indeed the
most comparative rascalliest sweet young prince. But Hal, I prithee
trouble me no more with vanity. I would to God thou and I knew   65
where a commodity of good names were to be bought. An old lord
of the Council rated me the other day in the street about you, sir,
but I marked him not, and yet he talked very wisely, but I regarded
him not, and yet he talked wisely – and in the street too.

Falstaff says that Hal has corrupted him, then claims that his god-given role in life is to steal. Poins and Hal joke at Falstaff's expense and Poins tells of a planned robbery.

1 Echoes of the Bible (in groups of three)

Lines 70–99 are filled with echoes of religion. Take parts and speak the lines in an exaggeratedly 'religious' way (for example, almost singing them in short sections, or echoing each short section, like responses of the congregation in a Christian church).

'Religious' words include: 'damnable', 'corrupt', 'saint', 'God', 'forgive', 'truly', 'wicked', 'Lord', 'Christendom', 'Zounds', 'amendment', 'hell', 'devil'.

Quotations or misquotations from the Bible include:

'wisdom cries out in the streets and no man regards it'

'I must give over this life' (echoing a sinner's wish to reform)

''Tis no sin for a man to labour in his vocation' (echoing 'Let every man abide in the same vocation wherein he was called')

'if men were to be saved by merit': Many Christians believed that salvation (going to heaven after death) was assured by 'merit' (good works)

'Remorse' (Poins' joking reference to Falstaff's mock repentance)

'Good Friday' – a strict fast day (that Falstaff ignores by eating and drinking).

2 A robbery is planned

Poins, like Hal, begins by jokingly insulting Falstaff. He then tells of the planned robbery at Gad's Hill (arranged by a highwayman called Gadshill). Turn to the map on page 2 to remind yourself of the location of the five places he mentions.

---

damnable iteration a devilish talent for misquoting the Bible
Zounds by God's wounds (a strong oath)
baffle me disgrace me, hang me upside down
set a match arranged a robbery

Stand! 'stand and deliver!' (a robbers' cry)
cozening cheating
vizards masks
bespoke ordered
tarry stay

PRINCE Thou didst well, for wisdom cries out in the streets and no   70
man regards it.

FALSTAFF O, thou hast damnable iteration, and art indeed able to
corrupt a saint. Thou hast done much harm upon me, Hal, God
forgive thee for it. Before I knew thee, Hal, I knew nothing, and
now am I, if a man should speak truly, little better than one of the   75
wicked. I must give over this life, and I will give it over. By the
Lord, an I do not I am a villain. I'll be damned for never a king's
son in Christendom.

PRINCE Where shall we take a purse tomorrow, Jack?

FALSTAFF Zounds, where thou wilt, lad, I'll make one; an I do not, call   80
me villain and baffle me.

PRINCE I see a good amendment of life in thee, from praying to purse-
taking.

FALSTAFF Why Hal, 'tis my vocation, Hal. 'Tis no sin for a man to
labour in his vocation.   85

Enter POINS

Poins! Now shall we know if Gadshill have set a match. O, if men
were to be saved by merit, what hole in hell were hot enough for
him? This is the most omnipotent villain that ever cried 'Stand!' to
a true man.

PRINCE Good morrow, Ned.   90

POINS Good morrow, sweet Hal. What says Monsieur Remorse?
What says Sir John Sack, and Sugar Jack? How agrees the devil
and thee about thy soul, that thou soldest him on Good Friday
last, for a cup of Madeira and a cold capon's leg?

PRINCE Sir John stands to his word, the devil shall have his bargain,   95
for he was never yet a breaker of proverbs. He will give the devil
his due.

POINS Then art thou damned for keeping thy word with the devil.

PRINCE Else he had been damned for cozening the devil.

POINS But my lads, my lads, tomorrow morning, by four o'clock early   100
at Gad's Hill, there are pilgrims going to Canterbury with rich
offerings and traders riding to London with fat purses. I have
vizards for you all; you have horses for yourselves. Gadshill lies
tonight in Rochester. I have bespoke supper tomorrow night in
Eastcheap. We may do it as secure as sleep. If you will go, I will   105
stuff your purses full of crowns. If you will not, tarry at home and
be hanged.

Hal refuses to join in the robbery. Falstaff leaves, hoping that Poins can persuade Hal to participate. Poins then tells Hal of his plan to rob Falstaff and the others once they have got the money.

From left to right: Hal, Poins, Falstaff. Choose a line from the script opposite as a suitable caption for this moment in the play.

1 Making an exit

As Falstaff leaves for the Boar's Head Tavern in London's Eastcheap, his parting lines 123–7 seem like a parody of a prayer. Try speaking the lines in a way to match your view of Falstaff's personality.

Yedward Edward (Poins)
chops fat cheeks
stand rob, fight
poor abuses thievery
want countenance lack
  sponsorship
latter spring old youngster

All-hallown summer Indian
  summer (a late summer; All-
  Hallows is 1 November)
waylaid ambushed
habits clothes
appointment item of equipment

FALSTAFF Hear ye, Yedward, if I tarry at home and go not, I'll hang
     you for going.

POINS You will, chops?

FALSTAFF Hal, wilt thou make one?

PRINCE Who I? Rob? I, a thief? Not I, by my faith.

FALSTAFF There's neither honesty, manhood, nor good fellowship in
     thee, nor thou camest not of the blood royal, if thou darest not
     stand for ten shillings.

PRINCE Well then, once in my days I'll be a madcap.

FALSTAFF Why, that's well said.

PRINCE Well, come what will, I'll tarry at home.

FALSTAFF By the Lord, I'll be a traitor then, when thou art king.

PRINCE I care not.

POINS Sir John, I prithee leave the Prince and me alone. I will lay him
     down such reasons for this adventure that he shall go.

FALSTAFF Well, God give thee the spirit of persuasion, and him the
     ears of profiting, that what thou speakest may move, and what he
     hears may be believed, that the true prince may – for recreation
     sake – prove a false thief, for the poor abuses of the time want
     countenance. Farewell, you shall find me in Eastcheap.

PRINCE Farewell, the latter spring! Farewell, All-hallown summer!

Exit Falstaff

POINS Now my good sweet honey lord, ride with us tomorrow. I have
     a jest to execute that I cannot manage alone. Falstaff, Peto,
     Bardolph, and Gadshill shall rob those men that we have already
     waylaid – yourself and I will not be there. And when they have the
     booty, if you and I do not rob them – cut this head off from my
     shoulders.

PRINCE How shall we part with them in setting forth?

POINS Why, we will set forth before or after them, and appoint them
     a place of meeting – wherein it is at our pleasure to fail – and then
     will they adventure upon the exploit themselves, which they shall
     have no sooner achieved but we'll set upon them.

PRINCE Yea, but 'tis like that they will know us by our horses, by our
     habits, and by every other appointment to be ourselves.

Poins explains the details of his plot, and says the fun will be in the lies Falstaff will tell. Alone on stage, Hal reveals his intention to change his behaviour to a more princely way of life.

1 What kind of friend? (in pairs)

What is Poins' relationship with Hal? In line 143, he addresses the Prince as 'sirrah', which can be used to a social superior ('Sir'), to a friend, or to a social inferior or child. Experiment with different ways of how Poins might speak 'sirrah', and how he delivers his exit line 154 ('Farewell, my lord') to suggest different kinds of attitudes to Hal.

2 Hal reveals his plan

In lines 155–77, Hal gives his reasons for joining in the low life of the tavern. By associating with Falstaff and his cronies he will gain a bad reputation. But when he throws off his loose behaviour, his reformation will appear more splendid, more glittering. It will be like the sun's appearance from behind 'contagious (infectious) clouds', or like an occasional and long wished-for holiday, or like bright metal on a dark background ('sullen ground'). When people least expect it, he will make up for all the time he has wasted.

a Because Hal's intention seems to be to use Falstaff and the others in the tavern merely to serve his own interests, he has been described as 'cold, calculating, hard-hearted and treacherous'. How far does each of these four adjectives match your view of him as revealed by the soliloquy?

b Work out a way of speaking the soliloquy that shows the audience your view of Hal's character.

---

cases of buckram suits of coarse cloth
nonce occasion
incomprehensible boundless, outrageous
wards sword-fencing styles
reproof disproof

unyoked humour unrestrained behaviour, wild tricks
wanted lacking, wished for
rare accidents unexpected events
foil contrast
Redeeming time making amends for wasted time

POINS Tut, our horses they shall not see, I'll tie them in the wood. Our
    vizards we will change after we leave them. And, sirrah, I have cases
    of buckram for the nonce, to immask our noted outward garments.
PRINCE Yea, but I doubt they will be too hard for us.　　　　　　　145
POINS Well, for two of them, I know them to be as true-bred cowards as
    ever turned back, and for the third, if he fight longer than he sees
    reason, I'll forswear arms. The virtue of this jest will be the incom-
    prehensible lies that this same fat rogue will tell us when we meet at
    supper. How thirty at least he fought with, what wards, what blows,　　150
    what extremities he endured, and in the reproof of this lives the jest.
PRINCE Well, I'll go with thee. Provide us all things necessary and
    meet me tomorrow night in Eastcheap. There I'll sup. Farewell.
POINS Farewell, my lord.

Exit Poins

PRINCE I know you all, and will a while uphold　　　　　　　　155
    The unyoked humour of your idleness.
    Yet herein will I imitate the sun,
    Who doth permit the base contagious clouds
    To smother up his beauty from the world,
    That when he please again to be himself,　　　　　　　　160
    Being wanted, he may be more wondered at
    By breaking through the foul and ugly mists
    Of vapours that did seem to strangle him.
    If all the year were playing holidays,
    To sport would be as tedious as to work;　　　　　　　　165
    But when they seldom come, they wished-for come,
    And nothing pleaseth but rare accidents.
    So when this loose behaviour I throw off,
    And pay the debt I never promisèd,
    By how much better than my word I am,　　　　　　　　170
    By so much shall I falsify men's hopes.
    And like bright metal on a sullen ground,
    My reformation, glitt'ring o'er my fault,
    Shall show more goodly, and attract more eyes
    Than that which hath no foil to set it off.　　　　　　　175
    I'll so offend, to make offence a skill,
    Redeeming time when men think least I will.　　　*Exit*

Henry demands fear and respect. He dismisses Worcester for reminding him that the Percy family helped him to power. Northumberland tries to excuse Hotspur's refusal to give up his prisoners.

1 Conflict (in small groups)

At the end of Scene 1, King Henry revealed that he has sent for Hotspur to explain his defiance in keeping the Scottish prisoners. Now the king and the Percy family come face to face. Smouldering resentment on both sides quickly bursts into conflict.

Imagine you are a theatre director. Your task is to stage lines 1–20 to greatest dramatic effect. Consider the following points:

- Opening stage direction: How can the entrance be staged to express the conflict of King Henry and the Percies before the first line is spoken?
- Is Henry instantly angry and confrontational, or might he speak his first nine lines in a calm and controlled way? Does he stand or sit, look directly at the Percies or avoid their eyes?
- Worcester claims that the Percy family ('Our house') does not deserve harsh treatment from the king, especially as they had helped him depose King Richard II and so become king himself. Suggest how Worcester can make every word count.
- Work out how Worcester makes his exit. Does he show or conceal his true feelings?

2 Respect

Only a display of strength will gain the respect of powerful people, claims Henry at line 9. Think of examples, from your own experience or from history or current affairs, which might prove or disprove Henry's claim.

Unapt to stir slow to be angered
condition recent manner
young down bird's small feathers
scourge of greatness punishment
 by the king
portly important, powerful

peremptory arrogant and
 dictatorial
moody frontier frowning
 appearance
misprision misunderstanding

ACT 1   SCENE 3
Windsor Castle

Enter the KING, NORTHUMBERLAND, WORCESTER, HOTSPUR,
SIR WALTER BLUNT, with others

KING My blood hath been too cold and temperate,
    Unapt to stir at these indignities,
    And you have found me – for accordingly
    You tread upon my patience. But be sure
    I will from henceforth rather be myself,   5
    Mighty, and to be feared, than my condition
    Which hath been smooth as oil, soft as young down,
    And therefore lost that title of respect,
    Which the proud soul ne'er pays but to the proud.
WORCESTER Our house, my sovereign liege, little deserves   10
    The scourge of greatness to be used on it,
    And that same greatness too which our own hands
    Have helped to make so portly.
NORTHUMBERLAND   My lord –
KING Worcester, get thee gone, for I do see
    Danger and disobedience in thine eye.   15
    O sir, your presence is too bold and peremptory,
    And majesty might never yet endure
    The moody frontier of a servant brow.
    You have good leave to leave us. When we need
    Your use and counsel we shall send for you.   20

Exit Worcester

[*To Northumberland*]
You were about to speak.
NORTHUMBERLAND   Yea, my good lord.
    Those prisoners in your highness' name demanded,
    Which Harry Percy here at Holmedon took,
    Were, as he says, not with such strength denied
    As is delivered to your majesty.   25
    Either envy therefore, or misprision,
    Is guilty of this fault, and not my son.

Hotspur explains that because he was so enraged by the pretentious and effeminate behaviour of King Henry's messenger, he simply cannot remember what he said to the demand for his prisoners.

1 What is Hotspur like? (in small groups)

Hotspur's story of the dandified lord reveals his own character as much as it does the courtier's. Rehearse and deliver Hotspur's lines, using some or all of the following suggestions:

a Pick out all the comparisons Hotspur uses to describe the courtier. Many are similes (comparisons using 'like' or 'as'): 'Fresh as a bridegroom', 'perfumèd like a milliner' (maker of women's hats and gloves) and so on. Does Hotspur speak each contemptuously?

b Identify where Hotspur may mimic the courtier's actual language: 'untaught knaves', 'unmannerly', 'slovenly unhandsome corpse', and so on.

c The king wants to know why Hotspur refused to give up his prisoners. Hotspur puts the blame on the courtier whose behaviour so irritated him. He tells that the courtier so exasperated him that he 'Answered neglectingly' (without thinking). Think carefully about lines 51–2 to decide what kind of answer Hotspur gave, and how he might speak those lines.

d Take parts as Hotspur and the courtier. As a third person speaks Hotspur's lines, act out the encounter between the two men.

e Hotspur is a soldier. The courtier represents everything he detests. Identify all the words Hotspur uses to express his irritation. Suggest why they represent the opposite of Hotspur's own values.

---

new reaped freshly shaved
stubble-land at harvest-home newly-harvested field
pouncet-box small box for herbs or snuff
holiday and lady unsoldierly and effeminate

popinjay noisy parrot
parmacity whale oil
saltpetre mineral used to make gunpowder
bald unjointed empty-headed irrelevant
Come current be held true

HOTSPUR My liege, I did deny no prisoners.
But I remember when the fight was done,
When I was dry with rage and extreme toil,   30
Breathless and faint, leaning upon my sword,
Came there a certain lord, neat and trimly dressed,
Fresh as a bridegroom, and his chin new reaped
Showed like a stubble-land at harvest-home.
He was perfumèd like a milliner,   35
And 'twixt his finger and his thumb he held
A pouncet-box, which ever and anon
He gave his nose, and took't away again –
Who therewith angry, when it next came there,
Took it in snuff. And still he smiled and talked;   40
And as the soldiers bore dead bodies by,
He called them untaught knaves, unmannerly,
To bring a slovenly unhandsome corpse
Betwixt the wind and his nobility.
With many holiday and lady terms   45
He questioned me, amongst the rest demanded
My prisoners in your majesty's behalf.
I then, all smarting with my wounds being cold,
To be so pestered with a popinjay,
Out of my grief and my impatience   50
Answered neglectingly, I know not what,
He should, or he should not, for he made me mad
To see him shine so brisk, and smell so sweet,
And talk so like a waiting-gentlewoman
Of guns, and drums, and wounds, God save the mark!   55
And telling me the sovereignest thing on earth
Was parmacity for an inward bruise,
And that it was great pity, so it was,
This villainous saltpetre should be digged
Out of the bowels of the harmless earth,   60
Which many a good tall fellow had destroyed
So cowardly, and but for these vile guns
He would himself have been a soldier.
This bald unjointed chat of his, my lord,
I answered indirectly, as I said,   65
And I beseech you, let not his report
Come current for an accusation
Betwixt my love and your high majesty.

23

Sir Walter Blunt justifies Hotspur's language, but King Henry rejects Hotspur's demand that Mortimer be ransomed in exchange for the prisoners. Hotspur defends Mortimer's loyalty and courage.

1 Blunt, the peacemaker

Sir Walter Blunt pleads to the king on Hotspur's behalf. Speak Blunt's lines in a manner you think might calm the king's anger.

2 Henry expresses his feelings (in pairs)

Hotspur, in telling his long story of the foppish courtier, has not spoken the full truth about the Scottish prisoners. As King Henry reveals, Hotspur wants to use the prisoners as a bargaining counter to secure the release of Mortimer ('that Earl of March'). That offer enrages Henry (for reasons given on pages 28–9).

Identify a word or phrase in each line that King Henry speaks that reveals the strength of his feelings about Hotspur, Mortimer or Glendower. Then speak the lines to each other giving your chosen words special emphasis. For example, in line 76, King Henry might stress 'Why' to show his exasperation and incredulity, and to express his rejection of Blunt's attempt at peacemaking.

3 Imagery and personification

a In line 86, Henry refuses to make a bargain with cowards ('indent with fears'). An indenture was a contract, which was torn in half. Each party kept a half. Fitting the two halves together proved the contract existed. Make a quick sketch to show such an indenture.

b Hotspur defends Mortimer's loyalty and bravery at the battle on the banks of the River Severn. He uses personification: giving the river the feelings and attributes of a human being. Find five or six ways in which personification is used in lines 103–5.

---

impeach accuse of disloyalty
unsay deny
But with proviso and exception except on the condition
charge expense
coffers treasure chests

fall off revolt
confound spend, waste
changing hardiment exchanging blows
breathed rested
crisp head rippling surface

BLUNT　The circumstance considered, good my lord,
　　　　Whate'er Lord Harry Percy then had said　　　　　70
　　　　To such a person, and in such a place,
　　　　At such a time, with all the rest retold,
　　　　May reasonably die, and never rise
　　　　To do him wrong, or any way impeach
　　　　What then he said, so he unsay it now.　　　　　75
KING　Why, yet he doth deny his prisoners,
　　　　But with proviso and exception,
　　　　That we at our own charge shall ransom straight
　　　　His brother-in-law, the foolish Mortimer,
　　　　Who, on my soul, hath wilfully betrayed　　　　　80
　　　　The lives of those that he did lead to fight
　　　　Against that great magician, damned Glendower,
　　　　Whose daughter, as we hear, that Earl of March
　　　　Hath lately married. Shall our coffers then
　　　　Be emptied to redeem a traitor home?　　　　　85
　　　　Shall we buy treason, and indent with fears
　　　　When they have lost and forfeited themselves?
　　　　No, on the barren mountains let him starve.
　　　　For I shall never hold that man my friend
　　　　Whose tongue shall ask me for one penny cost　　　90
　　　　To ransom home revolted Mortimer.
HOTSPUR　Revolted Mortimer!
　　　　He never did fall off, my sovereign liege,
　　　　But by the chance of war. To prove that true
　　　　Needs no more but one tongue for all those wounds,　　95
　　　　Those mouthèd wounds, which valiantly he took,
　　　　When on the gentle Severn's sedgy bank,
　　　　In single opposition, hand to hand,
　　　　He did confound the best part of an hour
　　　　In changing hardiment with great Glendower.　　　100
　　　　Three times they breathed, and three times did they drink
　　　　Upon agreement of swift Severn's flood,
　　　　Who then affrighted with their bloody looks
　　　　Ran fearfully among the trembling reeds,
　　　　And hid his crisp head in the hollow bank　　　　105
　　　　Bloodstained with these valiant combatants.

King Henry refuses to believe in Mortimer's courage. He again demands Hotspur's prisoners. Hotspur, restrained from confronting Henry, vows he will not give up his prisoners and will support Mortimer.

1 Henry asserts his authority

The antagonism between Henry and Hotspur bursts into open conflict as Henry accuses Hotspur of lying and again demands the Scottish prisoners.

a Speak King Henry's lines emphasising each word or phrase he probably intends as a threat, insult or rebuke. For example, in this confrontation, Henry's use of 'thou', 'thee' and 'sirrah' can express contempt.

b In his angry reply, Henry shifts from using 'I' and 'me' to the style that monarchs use to describe themselves: 'we' and 'us'. As you speak his lines, emphasise each pronoun, and think about why he changes his style.

2 Henry: ungrateful and fearful

Hotspur describes King Henry as 'this unthankful King', and as 'this ingrate (ungrateful) and cankered Bullingbrook'. His words express the resentment felt by the Percy family for Henry's treatment of them after they helped him (as Bullingbrook) to become king of England.

Hotspur notes how King Henry turned pale and trembled at the mention of Mortimer's name. Before you turn the page, make a guess about why Mortimer causes Henry so much anxiety.

---

policy trickery, craftiness
Colour her working disguise its deceits
belie tell lies about
durst dared
straight immediately

ease my heart express my true feelings
Albeit ... head Although I'm in danger of execution
choler anger
forsooth truly

Never did bare and rotten policy
Colour her working with such deadly wounds,
Nor never could the noble Mortimer
Receive so many, and all willingly.   110
Then let not him be slandered with revolt.
KING Thou dost belie him, Percy, thou dost belie him,
     He never did encounter with Glendower.
     I tell thee, he durst as well have met the devil alone
     As Owen Glendower for an enemy.   115
     Art thou not ashamed? But sirrah, henceforth
     Let me not hear you speak of Mortimer.
     Send me your prisoners with the speediest means –
     Or you shall hear in such a kind from me
     As will displease you. My Lord Northumberland: 120
     We license your departure with your son.
     Send us your prisoners, or you will hear of it.

Exit King [, with Blunt and train]

HOTSPUR And if the devil come and roar for them
     I will not send them. I will after straight
     And tell him so, for I will ease my heart,   125
     Albeit I make a hazard of my head.
NORTHUMBERLAND What? Drunk with choler? Stay, and pause a while,
     Here comes your uncle.

Enter WORCESTER

HOTSPUR   Speak of Mortimer?
     Zounds, I will speak of him, and let my soul
     Want mercy if I do not join with him.   130
     Yea, on his part I'll empty all these veins
     And shed my dear blood, drop by drop in the dust,
     But I will lift the down-trod Mortimer
     As high in the air as this unthankful King,
     As this ingrate and cankered Bullingbrook.   135
NORTHUMBERLAND Brother, the King hath made your nephew mad.
WORCESTER Who struck this heat up after I was gone?
HOTSPUR He will forsooth have all my prisoners,
     And when I urged the ransom once again
     Of my wife's brother, then his cheek looked pale,   140
     And on my face he turned an eye of death,
     Trembling even at the name of Mortimer.

*Worcester and Northumberland confirm that King Richard II declared
Mortimer as the next rightful king. Hotspur rebukes them for their
shameful part in Richard's fall and Henry's rise to power.*

1 Mortimer, the rightful king

The reason for King Henry's angry refusal to ransom Mortimer
becomes clear. Mortimer has a better claim to the throne of England
than Henry himself. Henry had deposed King Richard II and seized
the crown, but Richard had earlier declared Mortimer to be next in line
to become king. So Mortimer represents a very real threat to Henry,
who is all too aware of the doubtful legality of his kingship. Far better
for Henry if Mortimer is kept prisoner.

Inheritance in medieval England was governed by the law of
primogeniture: the crown passed to the male heir next in line ('next of
blood'). Turn to page 1: you will see that as a descendant of King
Edward III's second son, Mortimer, has a stronger claim than Henry,
whose father was Edward's third son.

Make your own copy of the family tree and keep it by you as you
work through the play. It will help you understand how family
relationships underpin the quarrel over the crown of England.

2 Home truths (in pairs)

Hotspur learns the reason why Henry so detests Mortimer (who is
Hotspur's brother-in-law, line 154). He rebukes his father and uncle
for the part they played, like hangmen, in Richard's overthrow and in
helping Henry to the throne. Work through Hotspur's lines 156–85 a
short section at a time, advising the actor how he might speak and
behave.

---

the world's wide mouth
  everybody's gossip
forgetful man Henry (who forgets
  the debt he owes to the Percy
  family)
detested blot foul stain
murderous subornation helping
  the murderer

base second means vile assistants
line and the predicament place
  and danger
range rank
chronicles history books
gage pledge, pawn

WORCESTER I cannot blame him. Was not he proclaimed,
    By Richard that dead is, the next of blood?
NORTHUMBERLAND He was, I heard the proclamation.   145
    And then it was, when the unhappy King –
    Whose wrongs in us God pardon! – did set forth
    Upon his Irish expedition;
    From whence he, intercepted, did return
    To be deposed, and shortly murderèd.   150
WORCESTER And for whose death we in the world's wide mouth
    Live scandalised and foully spoken of.
HOTSPUR But soft, I pray you, did King Richard then
    Proclaim my brother Edmund Mortimer
    Heir to the crown?
NORTHUMBERLAND   He did, myself did hear it.   155
HOTSPUR Nay then, I cannot blame his cousin King,
    That wished him on the barren mountains starve.
    But shall it be that you that set the crown
    Upon the head of this forgetful man,
    And for his sake wear the detested blot   160
    Of murderous subornation – shall it be
    That you a world of curses undergo,
    Being the agents, or base second means,
    The cords, the ladder, or the hangman rather?
    O pardon me, that I descend so low,   165
    To show the line and the predicament
    Wherein you range under this subtle King!
    Shall it for shame be spoken in these days,
    Or fill up chronicles in time to come,
    That men of your nobility and power   170
    Did gage them both in an unjust behalf –
    As both of you, God pardon it, have done –
    To put down Richard, that sweet lovely rose,
    And plant this thorn, this canker Bullingbrook?
    And shall it in more shame be further spoken,   175
    That you are fooled, discarded, and shook off
    By him for whom these shames ye underwent?

Hotspur urges his father and uncle to restore their tarnished reputations by challenging King Henry. Worcester hints at a dangerous secret plan, filling Hotspur with passionate thoughts of honour.

1 Honour (in small groups)

Hotspur is consumed with the notion of honour. In lines 178–84 he feels that his father and uncle have lost their honour ('banished honours') by supporting Henry's overthrow of King Richard. Worcester's talk of 'peril' rouses Hotspur into welcoming danger so that it can be met by honour (lines 192–6). The honourable man prefers to hunt the lion, not the hare.

In lines 199–206, Hotspur fantasises about recklessly rescuing honour from the distant moon or the deepest ocean, and so achieving honour totally for himself, not sharing in it with anyone else ('Without corrival' and in 'half-faced fellowship').

a Hotspur personifies honour as a female in lines 199–205. What picture of honour is conjured up in your mind by his imagery?

b Tell each other what you understand by honour. How different from each other's and from Hotspur's are your ideas about honour?

2 An image of danger

Worcester's plot will be as dangerous as a bridge made from a spear (lines 190–1). In medieval romance stories, knights proved their bravery by undertaking perilous tests, one of which was walking over a spear laid across a torrent. The image stirs Hotspur's imagination: if the knight falls off the spear-bridge, he will drown whether he can swim or not.

---

secret book plot
quick-conceiving discontents fast growing grievances
unsteadfast footing risky foothold
fathom-line line for measuring the depth of water
locks hair

redeem save, resume
out upon ... half-faced fellowship! I'll have nothing to do with sharing honour
apprehends a world ... attend sees an imaginary world, not reality

No, yet time serves wherein you may redeem
Your banished honours, and restore yourselves
Into the good thoughts of the world again: 180
Revenge the jeering and disdained contempt
Of this proud King, who studies day and night
To answer all the debt he owes to you,
Even with the bloody payment of your deaths.
Therefore, I say –

WORCESTER   Peace, cousin, say no more.   185
And now I will unclasp a secret book,
And to your quick-conceiving discontents
I'll read you matter deep and dangerous,
As full of peril and adventurous spirit
As to o'er-walk a current roaring loud   190
On the unsteadfast footing of a spear.

HOTSPUR If he fall in, good night, or sink, or swim!
Send danger from the east unto the west,
So honour cross it from the north to south,
And let them grapple. O, the blood more stirs   195
To rouse a lion than to start a hare!

NORTHUMBERLAND Imagination of some great exploit
Drives him beyond the bounds of patience.

[HOTSPUR] By heaven, methinks it were an easy leap
To pluck bright honour from the pale-faced moon,   200
Or dive into the bottom of the deep,
Where fathom-line could never touch the ground,
And pluck up drownèd honour by the locks,
So he that doth redeem her thence might wear
Without corrival all her dignities.   205
But out upon this half-faced fellowship!

WORCESTER He apprehends a world of figures here,
But not the form of what he should attend.
Good cousin, give me audience for a while.

HOTSPUR I cry you mercy.

Hotspur explodes at the thought of giving up his prisoners and says he will torment Henry with talk of Mortimer. Worcester and Northumberland tire of Hotspur's outbursts. Hotspur's anger makes him forgetful.

1 Views of Hal and Henry

Hotspur expresses the low public opinion of Prince Hal: 'that same sword-and-buckler Prince of Wales'. Swords and bucklers were the weapons and shields used by servants and braggarts. Hotspur is equally contemptuous of King Henry: 'this vile politician', 'this king of smiles'.

Keep Hotspur's descriptions in your mind as your read on, to see how much truth you think there is in his view of the royal son and father.

2 Hotspur in full flow!

Hotspur reveals more of his personality, furiously interrupting his uncle, planning further tricks to irritate Henry, and dismissing Prince Hal as a low-status unloved son. His anger at Henry (whom he calls Bullingbrook) makes him unable to remember the name of the place where they first met (you can find the episode which Hotspur describes in lines 239–49 in *Richard II* Act 2 Scene 3).

Northumberland calls Hotspur 'a wasp-stung and impatient fool'. Use that description, and everything that is conjured up in your mind by the nickname 'Hotspur', to help you speak everything Hotspur says opposite.

3 Repetition

Shakespeare knew that repeating words or phrases could be a very effective way of creating atmosphere and character. Pick out the repetitions in Hotspur's first two speeches opposite, and suggest how they help to deepen your understanding of what Hotspur is like.

scot tiny payment	**wasp-stung** irritated, tetchy
lend no ear do not listen	**scourged** flayed
still in motion always aroused	**pismires** ants
gall and pinch annoy and irritate	**'Sblood** By God's blood

WORCESTER   Those same noble Scots   210
    That are your prisoners –
HOTSPUR   I'll keep them all!
    By God he shall not have a scot of them,
    No, if a Scot would save his soul he shall not.
    I'll keep them, by this hand!
WORCESTER   You start away,
    And lend no ear unto my purposes.   215
    Those prisoners you shall keep –
HOTSPUR   Nay, I will. That's flat!
    He said he would not ransom Mortimer,
    Forbade my tongue to speak of Mortimer,
    But I will find him when he lies asleep,
    And in his ear I'll holla 'Mortimer!'   220
    Nay, I'll have a starling shall be taught to speak
    Nothing but 'Mortimer', and give it him
    To keep his anger still in motion.
WORCESTER Hear you, cousin, a word.
HOTSPUR All studies here I solemnly defy,   225
    Save how to gall and pinch this Bullingbrook.
    And that same sword-and-buckler Prince of Wales –
    But that I think his father loves him not
    And would be glad he met with some mischance –
    I would have him poisoned with a pot of ale.   230
WORCESTER Farewell, kinsman. I'll talk to you
    When you are better tempered to attend.
NORTHUMBERLAND Why, what a wasp-stung and impatient fool
    Art thou to break into this woman's mood,
    Tying thine ear to no tongue but thine own!   235
HOTSPUR Why, look you, I am whipped and scourged with rods,
    Nettled, and stung with pismires, when I hear
    Of this vile politician Bullingbrook.
    In Richard's time – what do you call the place?
    A plague upon it, it is in Gloucestershire.   240
    'Twas where the madcap Duke his uncle kept –
    His uncle York – where I first bowed my knee
    Unto this king of smiles, this Bullingbrook –
    'Sblood, when you and he came back from Ravenspurgh –
NORTHUMBERLAND At Berkeley Castle.

Hotspur mocks King Henry's praise of him at their first meeting.
Worcester tells Hotspur to give up his prisoners and reveals a growing
rebellion against King Henry.

1 False flattery (in pairs)

Hotspur mimics Henry's flattering words when first they met. Speak the phrases that Hotspur imitates (lines 248–9). Then talk together about how effective you feel 'candy' and 'fawning greyhound' to be as descriptions of false flattery.

2 Worcester's plan

Worcester reveals his plan for rebellion against Henry. Hotspur is to free his Scottish prisoners without ransom. In so doing he will gain their goodwill and make them allies. At the same time, Northumberland is to befriend the Archbishop of York who is also plotting rebellion because Henry executed his relative, Lord Scroop.

Imagine yourself as Worcester and write the notes he made for the plot in which he sets out the action to be taken and the reasons for those actions. Use lines 254–70 and lines 277–93 as your inspiration.

3 Can't keep a secret?

Northumberland's line 272 shows he is well aware of his son's impetuous behaviour, and fears that Hotspur will recklessly reveal the plot. He uses an image from hunting, prompted by Hotspur's 'I smell it'. Hotspur is like a hound catching the scent of a fox or deer, but Northumberland fears that before the hunted animal is really in view ('the game is afoot'), Hotspur will release his hounds ('let'st slip').

Glance back at each of Northumberland's speeches in this scene. Identify the various ways in which he describes his son.

---

candy deal sweet flattering amount
fawning greyhound falsely fond dog
cozeners cheats
stay your leisure wait until you've finished

divers many and various (diverse)
into the bosom creep become a trusted friend
prelate churchman
in estimation as a guess
ruminated thought about

HOTSPUR   You say true.   245
        Why, what a candy deal of courtesy
        This fawning greyhound then did proffer me!
        'Look when his infant fortune came to age',
        And 'gentle Harry Percy', and 'kind cousin'.
        O, the devil take such cozeners – God forgive me!   250
        Good uncle, tell your tale. I have done.
WORCESTER Nay, if you have not, to it again,
        We will stay your leisure.
HOTSPUR   I have done, i'faith.
WORCESTER Then once more to your Scottish prisoners.
        Deliver them up without their ransom straight,   255
        And make the Douglas' son your only mean
        For powers in Scotland, which, for divers reasons
        Which I shall send you written, be assured
        Will easily be granted. [*To Northumberland*] You my lord,
        Your son in Scotland being thus employed,   260
        Shall secretly into the bosom creep
        Of that same noble prelate well-beloved,
        The Archbishop.
HOTSPUR   Of York, is it not?
WORCESTER True, who bears hard
        His brother's death at Bristol, the Lord Scroop.   265
        I speak not this in estimation,
        As what I think might be, but what I know
        Is ruminated, plotted, and set down,
        And only stays but to behold the face
        Of that occasion that shall bring it on.   270
HOTSPUR I smell it! Upon my life it will do well!
NORTHUMBERLAND Before the game is afoot thou still let'st slip.
HOTSPUR Why, it cannot choose but be a noble plot;
        And then the power of Scotland, and of York,
        To join with Mortimer, ha?
WORCESTER   And so they shall.   275
HOTSPUR In faith it is exceedingly well aimed.

Worcester urges speed in the rebellion because he thinks that King Henry, fearing the Percy family, will have them executed. Worcester plans to co-ordinate the rebellion. Hotspur longs for action.

1 Three leading rebels (in groups of three)

Northumberland, Worcester and Hotspur (father, brother, son) are the three members of the Percy family who will lead the revolt against King Henry. Look back over Scene 3 and find a few short quotations that you think are characteristic of each man. For example, Hotspur's final line opposite suggests much about him. He longs for battlefields, fighting, and the cries of dying men, describing them all as 'sport'.

Use your quotations to write a paragraph for each character in order to guide the actor playing the part.

2 Scene 3 in two minutes (in small groups)

Here's one way of identifying the different sections of Scene 3:

lines 1–20: the dismissal of Worcester

lines 21–76: the Scottish prisoners

lines 77–122: Mortimer

lines 123–251: Hotspur's anger and imagination

lines 252–96: Worcester's plot

Use these five sections (or make up your own divisions of the scene) to create a very short version of the scene using only two or three of Shakespeare's lines from each section.

3 'No further go in this'

How might Worcester speak line 286 to Hotspur? Give reasons for your reply.

---

raising of a head recruiting an army
even carefully, peacefully
pay us home execute us

Cousin (in Shakespeare's time it was customary to call any close relative 'cousin')
suddenly very soon
fashion organise
fields battlefields

WORCESTER And 'tis no little reason bids us speed,
   To save our heads by raising of a head.
   For, bear ourselves as even as we can,
   The King will always think him in our debt,   280
   And think we think ourselves unsatisfied,
   Till he hath found a time to pay us home.
   And see already how he doth begin
   To make us strangers to his looks of love.
HOTSPUR He does, he does, we'll be revenged on him.   285
WORCESTER Cousin, farewell. No further go in this
   Than I by letters shall direct your course.
   When time is ripe, which will be suddenly,
   I'll steal to Glendower and Lord Mortimer,
   Where you, and Douglas, and our powers at once,   290
   As I will fashion it, shall happily meet
   To bear our fortunes in our own strong arms,
   Which now we hold at much uncertainty.
NORTHUMBERLAND Farewell, good brother. We shall thrive, I trust.
HOTSPUR Uncle, adieu. O, let the hours be short,   295
   Till fields, and blows, and groans applaud our sport!

                Exeunt

Looking back at Act 1
Activities for groups or individuals

1 Disorder threatens

In Scenes 1, 2 and 3 disorder threatens. Henry's conscience is disturbed; there are attacks from Wales and from Scotland; rebellion is planned by the Percies of the North. In the tavern, the Prince of Wales idles away his time with thieves planning a robbery. What worries King Henry most? Make a list of all that troubles him and put it in order of importance to him.

2 Dramatic construction

Shakespeare presents alternating scenes of the three groups of characters: court, tavern and rebels. The alternating pattern provides all kinds of contrasts. For example, Scene 1 ends emphasising 'speed'; Scene 2 opens with Hal's dismissal of the importance of time. As you work through the play, you will find that this alternating pattern continues (see pages 10, 150 and 185). You will also find activities to help you understand how this juxtaposition of scenes heightens dramatic effect, and adds to the significance of such themes as honour, order and disorder, England, Hal's education, and so on.

3 Political diary

Imagine you are King Henry's political secretary. Your job each day is to write up an account of political happenings. Write your report of what happens in Scenes 1 and 3.

4 Scene locations

On the open Elizabethan stage there were no elaborate sets. One scene flowed quickly into the next. In this edition, locations are given for each scene, but no-one really knows for certain where Shakespeare intended every scene to be set. For example, Scene 2 might be set in a street, a room in the Prince's apartments, or a London tavern. In the modern theatre scenes also flow quickly into each other, but there is usually a set design that can be speedily changed to represent a different location. Design a simple set that can swiftly change to show the three different locations in Act 1.

'So shaken as we are, so wan with care.' King Henry is all too aware of his insecure hold on the crown of England. How closely does this portrayal match your own imagined picture of the king?

5 Scene openings

The opening 'business' (stage activity) of a scene can create atmosphere and character before the first line is spoken. For example, one production staged the opening of Scene 1 with Henry stumbling as he approached the throne (to signify his doubtful right to be king); at the start of Scene 2, Hal woke Falstaff by throwing a pot of ale in his face.

Work out how to stage the openings of Scenes 1, 2 and 3 to give an unspoken indication of character and theme.

Two Carriers, preparing for their journey, criticise conditions at the inn: bad fodder for the horses, flea-ridden rooms, no chamber pots. The First Carrier curses the stableman for slackness.

1 Act it out! (in groups of three)

In the yard of a run-down inn, two Carriers prepare to take their goods on the twenty-mile journey to London. They have spent an uncomfortable night, and the stableman of the inn neglects his duties.

Carriers used horses with panniers or saddlebags to transport goods around England. They were the equivalent of today's truck drivers. Just as a driver looks after his truck, so carriers were concerned about their horses. In lines 5–6, the First Carrier instructs the Ostler (stableman) to soften his pack horse's saddle by beating it and stuffing the pommel with wool ('a few flocks in the point'), because the worn out horse ('jade') is excessively sore around the shoulders ('wrung in the withers, out of all cess').

Take parts as the First and Second Carrier, and as Gadshill (who can also speak the Ostler's line 4). Rehearse and act out lines 1–37. Think about accents for the Carriers, and how you can convey to the audience that it is early morning and still dark. Work out stage 'business' (in some productions the Second Carrier catches and examines a flea at line 13). The following explanation of names may help you:

'Charles' Wain' (line 2) – Charlemagne's Wagon, a nickname for the Plough (the star constellation Ursa Major also known as the Bear or the Big Dipper)

'Robin Ostler' (line 9) – a stableman who once worked at the inn

'king Christian' (line 14) – probably the Carrier means a Christian King

'Cut' (line 5) – name of the packhorse with a cut tail

dank damp and cold	**leak** urinate
bots worms in intestines	**chamber-lye** urine
tench fish with red markings (believed to be flea-bitten)	**loach** a type of fish (believed to breed lice)
first cock midnight (first cockcrow)	**races** roots
jordan chamber pot	**pate** head

Act 2 Scene 1

An inn yard in Rochester

Enter a CARRIER *with a lantern in his hand*

FIRST CARRIER Heigh-ho! An it be not four by the day I'll be hanged. Charles' Wain is over the new chimney, and yet our horse not packed. What, Ostler!

OSTLER [*Within*] Anon, anon.

FIRST CARRIER I prithee, Tom, beat Cut's saddle, put a few flocks in the point; poor jade is wrung in the withers, out of all cess. 5

Enter another CARRIER

SECOND CARRIER Peas and beans are as dank here as a dog, and that is the next way to give poor jades the bots. This house is turned upside down since Robin Ostler died.

FIRST CARRIER Poor fellow never joyed since the price of oats rose, it was the death of him. 10

SECOND CARRIER I think this be the most villainous house in all London road for fleas, I am stung like a tench.

FIRST CARRIER Like a tench! By the mass, there is ne'er a king Christian could be better bit than I have been since the first cock. 15

SECOND CARRIER Why, they will allow us ne'er a jordan, and then we leak in your chimney, and your chamber-lye breeds fleas like a loach.

FIRST CARRIER What, Ostler! Come away, and be hanged, come away!

SECOND CARRIER I have a gammon of bacon, and two races of ginger, to be delivered as far as Charing Cross. 20

FIRST CARRIER God's body! The turkeys in my pannier are quite starved. What, Ostler! A plague on thee, hast thou never an eye in thy head? Canst not hear? An 'twere not as good deed as drink to break the pate on thee, I am a very villain. Come and be hanged! Hast no faith in thee? 25

The Carriers are suspicious of Gadshill and answer his questions evasively. The Chamberlain reports on the rich travellers about to depart. Gadshill forecasts the robbery.

1 Don't trust Gadshill

Gadshill is a 'setter', a person who organises a theft. He is named after Gad's Hill, a notorious place for robberies on the London to Canterbury road. The two Carriers seem to think that he is a suspicious character. They tell him the wrong time, refuse him a lantern, and avoid telling him when they will arrive in London.

What is it about Gadshill that arouses their suspicion? Write a paragraph about his appearance, movements, speaking style, and so on.

2 And don't trust the Chamberlain

Like the American wagon trains of the nineteenth century, travellers in Shakespeare's time (and in the time of King Henry), rode together in 'company' (line 37). There was safety in numbers. But there were also plenty of untrustworthy people ready to betray information about travellers to thieves. The Chamberlain is the manager of the inn, and he has already told Gadshill of rich pickings ('abundance of charge') from the company who stayed overnight.

This is the Chamberlain's only appearance, and he has only fifteen lines. Suggest how an actor can make this small role memorable in a way that will help the audience to understand what the Chamberlain contributes to the play.

3 Saint Nicholas

Saint Nicholas, the patron saint of travellers, children and scholars, was also the patron saint of thieves. So 'Saint Nicholas' clerks' (line 49) are highwaymen. In English slang, to 'nick' is to steal, and to behave 'nickishly' is to be deceitful and dishonest.

---

gelding castrated horse
soft just a minute
Marry By the Virgin Mary
Mugs the First Carrier's name?
quoth pick-purse says the pickpocket

holds current is still true
franklin rich yeoman
three hundred marks £200
auditor king's officer who checked accounts
presently immediately

Enter GADSHILL

GADSHILL Good morrow, carriers, what's o'clock?

[FIRST] CARRIER I think it be two o'clock.

GADSHILL I prithee lend me thy lantern, to see my gelding in the stable.

FIRST CARRIER Nay, by God, soft! I know a trick worth two of that, 30
    i'faith.

GADSHILL I pray thee lend me thine.

SECOND CARRIER Ay, when? Canst tell? Lend me thy lantern, quoth he!
    Marry I'll see thee hanged first.

GADSHILL Sirrah carrier, what time do you mean to come to London?

SECOND CARRIER Time enough to go to bed with a candle, I warrant 35
    thee! Come, neighbour Mugs, we'll call up the gentlemen, they will
    along with company, for they have great charge.

Exeunt [*Carriers*]

GADSHILL What ho! Chamberlain!

Enter CHAMBERLAIN

CHAMBERLAIN 'At hand, quoth pick-purse.'

GADSHILL That's even as fair as 'At hand, quoth the chamberlain', for 40
    thou variest no more from picking of purses than giving direction
    doth from labouring. Thou layest the plot how.

CHAMBERLAIN Good morrow, Master Gadshill. It holds current that I
    told you yesternight. There's a franklin in the Weald of Kent hath
    brought three hundred marks with him in gold – I heard him tell it 45
    to one of his company last night at supper, a kind of auditor, one
    that hath abundance of charge too, God knows what. They are up
    already, and call for eggs and butter. They will away presently.

GADSHILL Sirrah, if they meet not with Saint Nicholas' clerks, I'll give
    thee this neck. 50

CHAMBERLAIN No, I'll none of it, I pray thee keep that for the hangman,
    for I know thou worshippest Saint Nicholas, as truly as a man of
    falsehood may.

Gadshill boasts of his rich and powerful friends, who are not like common thieves. He is confident of escaping punishment and claims to be a true man, promising the Chamberlain a share of the stolen money.

1 The 'profession' of thieves

Gadshill boasts that his fellow robbers are not ordinary thieves, but persons of high status. He names Falstaff, and broadly hints at Prince Hal and Poins ('other Troyans' means other drinking partners). Their high rank gives grace to 'the profession' (fellow thieves). Gadshill lists some common villains:

'foot-landrakers' (line 59) – poor thieves who cannot afford a horse

'long-staff sixpenny strikers' (line 60) – robbers who used long poles with iron hooks to pull travellers off their horses, for tiny amounts of money

'mustachio purple-hued maltworms' (line 61) – red-faced drunkards with huge moustaches

To contrast with these poor thieves, Gadshill boasts he is joined with 'nobility and tranquillity, burgomasters and great oneyres'. But who are 'oneyres'? The word may be an error by a printer, making a guess at Shakespeare's handwriting. Many alterations have been made: 'moneyers', 'owners', 'honeyeres', 'one-yers', 'seignors', 'mynheers', 'oyezers'. No one really knows, so give your own idea of what Shakespeare might have had in mind for 'great oneyres'.

2 An important scene?

Some people have felt that Scene 1 is a very unimportant episode, not worthy of Shakespeare. Others consider it very significant to an appreciation of the play. Suggest what you think it contributes to the picture of England presented by the play; to audience entertainment; to an understanding of themes (see pages 186–9); and how it develops the plot of the play.

---

tranquillity peacemakers (or is Gadshill simply rhyming for effect?)
burgomasters town magistrates
commonwealth wealth of society
boots booty, stolen goods
liquored greased, made drunk

cock-sure with confidence in our safety
receipt of fern-seed recipe for invisibility (a folk belief)
homo man (I'm a man like all others)

GADSHILL What talkest thou to me of the hangman? If I hang, I'll make
a fat pair of gallows. For if I hang, old Sir John hangs with me, and   55
thou knowest he is no starveling. Tut, there are other Troyans that
thou dreamest not of, the which for sport sake are content to do the
profession some grace, that would, if matters should be looked into,
for their own credit sake make all whole. I am joined with no foot-
landrakers, no long-staff sixpenny strikers, none of these mad   60
mustachio purple-hued maltworms, but with nobility and tranquillity, burgomasters and great oneyres, such as can hold in, such as will
strike sooner than speak, and speak sooner than drink, and drink
sooner than pray. And yet, zounds, I lie, for they pray continually to
their saint the commonwealth, or rather not pray to her, but prey on   65
her, for they ride up and down on her, and make her their boots.
CHAMBERLAIN What, the commonwealth their boots? Will she hold
out water in foul way?
GADSHILL She will, she will, justice hath liquored her. We steal as in
a castle, cock-sure. We have the receipt of fern-seed, we walk   70
invisible.
CHAMBERLAIN Nay, by my faith, I think you are more beholding to the
night than to fern-seed for your walking invisible.
GADSHILL Give me thy hand, thou shalt have a share in our purchase,
as I am a true man.   75
CHAMBERLAIN Nay, rather let me have it as you are a false thief.
GADSHILL Go to, *homo* is a common name to all men. Bid the ostler
bring my gelding out of the stable. Farewell, you muddy knave.

[Exeunt]

Poins keeps out of sight of Falstaff who curses him for hiding his horse. Falstaff threatens Poins with death, and regrets that neither Hal nor Poins are true to him.

1 Enact the scene (in groups of eight or more)

A major aim of this scene is to make the audience laugh as much as possible. Take parts, do a first read through, then rehearse a performance to help your audience get the verbal jokes as well as enjoying the physical action. Keep in mind the following:

- It is a very dark night.
- Falstaff is very fat and short of breath.
- The pace of different sections of the scene.

Falstaff nearly always tries to turn everything that is said to him into a joke. But is he serious in parts of this scene?

2 'Frets like a gummed velvet'

Poins' image that Falstaff 'frets like a gummed velvet' describes Falstaff's irritation. The precise meaning is unclear to most members of a modern audience. In Shakespeare's time, velvet was stiffened by coating it with gum (glue), which made it wear away. In one production Poins pulled a face and felt around his neck as if it was chafed by a very stiff collar.

Make a suggestion of your own for some stage business to help the audience to understand the image.

3 'Whew!'

What does Falstaff do at line 24? Some actors get a laugh by having Falstaff unable to whistle, however hard he tries.

---

steps to one side hides at edge of stage
by the square precisely (a 'square' was a measuring instrument)
forsworn sworn to abandon

medicines drugs
veriest varlet poorest servant, greatest rogue
threescore-and-ten seventy

ACT 2 SCENE 2
The road at Gad's Hill

Enter PRINCE, POINS, and PETO with BARDOLPH

POINS Come, shelter, shelter! I have removed Falstaff's horse, and he
frets like a gummed velvet.

PRINCE Stand close!

[They retire]

Enter FALSTAFF

FALSTAFF Poins! Poins, and be hanged! Poins!

PRINCE [*Coming forward*] Peace, ye fat-kidneyed rascal, what a brawling   5
dost thou keep!

FALSTAFF Where's Poins, Hal?

PRINCE He is walked up to the top of the hill. I'll go seek him.

[He steps to one side]

FALSTAFF I am accursed to rob in that thief's company. The rascal hath
removed my horse and tied him I know not where. If I travel but   10
four foot by the square further afoot, I shall break my wind. Well,
I doubt not but to die a fair death for all this, if I scape hanging for
killing that rogue. I have forsworn his company hourly any time this
two-and-twenty years, and yet I am bewitched with the rogue's
company. If the rascal have not given me medicines to make me   15
love him, I'll be hanged. It could not be else. I have drunk medicines.
Poins! Hal! A plague upon you both! Bardolph! Peto! I'll starve ere
I'll rob a foot further – an 'twere not as good a deed as drink to turn
true man, and to leave these rogues, I am the veriest varlet that ever
chewed with a tooth. Eight yards of uneven ground is threescore-   20
and-ten miles afoot with me, and the stony-hearted villains know it
well enough. A plague upon it when thieves cannot be true one to
another!

They whistle

Whew! A plague upon you all. Give me my horse you rogues, give
me my horse and be hanged!   25

Falstaff complains that Hal is fooling him and threatens to mock the Prince in song. As the thieves prepare for the robbery, Falstaff denies that he is a coward.

1 Write the ballad (in pairs)

Falstaff tells Hal to hang himself in his own Order of the Garter (which Hal would wear as next in line to the throne). He then threatens to have a rude ballad written to mock the Prince and Poins. In Shakespeare's time, ballads were very popular and it was possible to hire a writer to compose a ballad to ridicule an enemy or rival.

When you have finished reading and acting the scene, write your own 'Ballad of Gadshill' as if you had been hired by Falstaff to make fun of Hal and Poins.

2 Is Falstaff a coward?

For many years people have argued fiercely over whether Falstaff is or is not a coward. As you work through the play, you will find plenty of evidence to help you make up your own mind about Falstaff's bravery – or lack of it. Begin by thinking about lines 50–6 opposite.

When Falstaff learns there are eight or ten travellers he asks 'Zounds, will they not rob us?'. Hal questions his bravery and calls him 'Sir John Paunch'. Falstaff makes a punning reply, using Hal's grandfather's name to suggest he is not gaunt (thin). He then denies he is a coward.

Speak line 52 and lines 54–5 in a way that shows whether or not you think Falstaff really is a coward.

---

list listen
'Sblood By God's blood
exchequer treasury
colt trick, fool
uncolted unhorsed
taken captured, arrested
peach turn informer

setter accomplice who has arranged a robbery
Case ye put on your masks
vizards face masks
front confront
light on meet

PRINCE [*Coming forward*] Peace, ye fat-guts, lie down, lay thine ear
close to the ground and list if thou canst hear the tread of travellers.

FALSTAFF Have you any levers to lift me up again, being down?
'Sblood, I'll not bear my own flesh so far afoot again for all the coin
in thy father's exchequer. What a plague mean ye to colt me thus?   30

PRINCE Thou liest, thou art not colted, thou art uncolted.

FALSTAFF I prithee good Prince, help me to my horse, good king's son.

PRINCE Out ye rogue, shall I be your ostler?

FALSTAFF Hang thyself in thine own heir-apparent garters! If I be
taken, I'll peach for this. An I have not ballads made on you all, and   35
sung to filthy tunes, let a cup of sack be my poison. When a jest is
so forward – and afoot too – I hate it!

Enter GADSHILL

GADSHILL Stand!

FALSTAFF So I do, against my will.

POINS [*Coming forward with Bardolph and Peto*] O, 'tis our setter, I   40
know his voice. Bardolph, what news?

BARDOLPH Case ye, case ye, on with your vizards, there's money of the
King's coming down the hill. 'Tis going to the King's exchequer.

[*They put on visors*]

FALSTAFF You lie, ye rogue, 'tis going to the King's tavern.

GADSHILL There's enough to make us all –   45

FALSTAFF To be hanged.

PRINCE Sirs, you four shall front them in the narrow lane. Ned Poins
and I will walk lower – if they scape from your encounter, then they
light on us.

PETO How many be there of them?   50

GADSHILL Some eight or ten.

FALSTAFF Zounds, will they not rob us?

PRINCE What, a coward, Sir John Paunch?

FALSTAFF Indeed, I am not John of Gaunt your grandfather, but yet no
coward, Hal.   55

PRINCE Well, we leave that to the proof.

POINS Sirrah Jack, thy horse stands behind the hedge. When thou
need'st him, there thou shalt find him. Farewell, and stand fast!

FALSTAFF Now cannot I strike him, if I should be hanged.

PRINCE [*Aside to Poins*] Ned, where are our disguises?   60

POINS Here, hard by, stand close.

[*Exeunt Prince and Poins*]

Falstaff and his companions rob the travellers. As they prepare to share out their booty they are set upon by Hal and Poins and put to flight, leaving their ill-gotten gains behind.

1 Staging the robberies

Every new production of the play spends a long time planning and rehearsing how the complicated action on the opposite page can be staged. The aim is to make the double robbery as funny as possible for the audience. There is much coming and going, and practical problems to be solved about just how each robbery is performed.

A key problem is how Falstaff behaves when he is robbed by Hal and Poins. Does he act like a complete coward? Or does he put up a convincing show of bravery in the 'blow or two' (stage direction, line 85) he hands out before running away?

Work out your own staging of what happens. Ensure that the audience can understand and enjoy the action.

2 Who is he describing?

One student playing Falstaff said about his language as he robs the travellers: 'People in glass houses shouldn't throw stones. Most of the things Falstaff calls the travellers apply to himself!'. Suggest why Falstaff uses such insults in lines 68–75. Do they describe himself?

---

happy man be his dole may the outcome be happy for us all
whoreson caterpillars wretched parasites
fleece rob
gorbellied pot-bellied
chuffs rich misers

store entire wealth
grandjurors rich jurymen
jure (Falstaff invents a threat)
argument the topic of conversation
no equity stirring no justice in the world

FALSTAFF Now, my masters, happy man be his dole, say I. Every man
to his business.

Enter the TRAVELLERS

[FIRST] TRAVELLER Come, neighbour, the boy shall lead our horses
down the hill. We'll walk afoot a while and ease our legs.   65
THIEVES Stand!
[SECOND] TRAVELLER Jesus bless us!
FALSTAFF Strike, down with them, cut the villains' throats! Ah,
whoreson caterpillars, bacon-fed knaves, they hate us youth! Down
with them, fleece them!   70
[FIRST] TRAVELLER O, we are undone, both we and ours for ever!
FALSTAFF Hang ye, gorbellied knaves, are ye undone? No, ye fat chuffs,
I would your store were here! On, bacons, on! What, ye knaves,
young men must live! You are grandjurors, are ye? We'll jure ye,
faith.   75
Here they rob them and bind them

Exeunt

Enter the PRINCE *and* POINS [, *disguised*]

PRINCE The thieves have bound the true men. Now, could thou and I
rob the thieves, and go merrily to London, it would be argument for
a week, laughter for a month, and a good jest for ever.
POINS Stand close, I hear them coming.

[*They retire*]

Enter the thieves again

FALSTAFF Come, my masters, let us share, and then to horse before day.   80
An the Prince and Poins be not two arrant cowards there's no
equity stirring. There's no more valour in that Poins than in a wild
duck.
As they are sharing the PRINCE *and* POINS *set upon them*

PRINCE Your money!
POINS Villains!   85
They all run away, and Falstaff after a blow or two runs away too,
leaving the booty behind them

Delighted with the success of their plan, Hal and Poins laugh at Falstaff's discomfort. In Scene 3, Hotspur is angered by a letter from a lord who refuses to join the rebellion.

1 Fat Falstaff

Hal uses a striking image in lines 90–1: 'Falstaff sweats to death, And lards the lean earth as he walks along'. Suggest what picture it calls up in your mind, then quickly look back through Scene 2 to remind yourself of all the references to Falstaff's size.

2 Change of scene

From the open road at Gad's Hill, the scene shifts to Warkworth Castle in Northumberland. In Shakespeare's theatre the action flowed quickly from one scene to another without elaborate set changes (see Activity 4 page 38). Imagine you are directing the play on a bare stage, but you wish to signal the change of location by means of one or two simple props or symbols. Sketch your solution.

3 Caution and anger (in pairs)

Hotspur reads a letter from a lord who is never named. Much to Hotspur's annoyance, the unknown lord refuses to join the rebellion. Read aloud lines 1–29, with one person speaking as the letter writer (the lines in italic). The other responds as Hotspur who puts as much contempt as possible into his lines.

Afterwards, talk together about what Hotspur's response shows about his character. For example the image in lines 7–9 echoes an old country belief: a stinging nettle does not sting if it is firmly grasped. Hotspur believes in meeting danger with brave action: whatever the peril, bold response will ensure success.

---

officer constable	**for the counterpoise of** to balance, outweigh
house family	
take a cold catch a cold	**hind** female deer, servant, peasant
uncertain unreliable	**expectation** hope
unsorted unsuitable, badly chosen	**Lord of York** Archbishop of York

PRINCE Got with much ease. Now merrily to horse.
    The thieves are all scattered and possessed with fear
    So strongly that they dare not meet each other.
    Each takes his fellow for an officer!
    Away, good Ned! Falstaff sweats to death,   90
    And lards the lean earth as he walks along.
    Were it not for laughing I should pity him.
POINS How the fat rogue roared!

Exeunt

ACT 2   SCENE 3
Warkworth Castle

Enter HOTSPUR *reading a letter*

[HOTSPUR] '*But for mine own part, my lord, I could be well contented to be
    there, in respect of the love I bear your house.*'
    He could be contented! Why is he not then? In respect of the love
    he bears our house. He shows in this he loves his own barn better
    than he loves our house. Let me see some more.   5
    '*The purpose you undertake is dangerous,*'
    Why, that's certain. 'Tis dangerous to take a cold, to sleep, to drink.
    But I tell you, my lord fool, out of this nettle, danger, we pluck this
    flower, safety.
    '*The purpose you undertake is dangerous, the friends you have named*   10
    uncertain, the time itself unsorted, and your whole plot too light, for the
    counterpoise of so great an opposition.'
    Say you so, say you so? I say unto you again, you are a shallow
    cowardly hind, and you lie. What a lack-brain is this! By the Lord,
    our plot is a good plot, as ever was laid, our friends true and   15
    constant. A good plot, good friends, and full of expectation. An
    excellent plot, very good friends. What a frosty-spirited rogue is
    this! Why, my Lord of York commends the plot, and the general
    course of the action. Zounds, an I were now by this rascal I could
    brain him with his lady's fan. Is there not my father, my uncle, and   20
    myself? Lord Edmund Mortimer, my Lord of York, and Owen

Hotspur dismisses the fear that the unknown lord will betray the rebels' plans to King Henry. Hotspur's wife tells of his distractedness and bad dreams. She demands to know what worries him.

1 The unknown lord

No one knows the identity of the letter-writer. Hotspur despises his caution, calling it cowardice, and suspects he will reveal ('lay open') the rebels' plans to King Henry. Invent an identity for the unknown lord and write his letter to the king, telling what you know of Hotspur's plot.

2 A wife's view of Hotspur (in small groups)

Lady Percy gives a vivid account of Hotspur's behaviour. She reveals a very different picture of the man who talks boldly and confidently about danger and rebellion. She sees someone who, waking and sleeping, is filled with disturbed thoughts and visions.

Explore ways of speaking her lines to intensify dramatic effect. For example, one student can play Hotspur; the others stand or sit in a circle around Hotspur and share Kate's speech, each speaking only a small section before handing on to the next speaker. Hotspur mimes each section as it is spoken. You will find help with the language below and at the foot of the page.

'terms of manage' (line 43) – words of horsemanship

'field' (line 44) – battlefield

'sallies, and retires' (line 45) – attacks and retreats

'palisadoes, frontiers' (line 46) – defences of sharpened stakes, ramparts

'basilisks' (line 47) – large cannons

'culverin' (line 47) – small cannons

'currents' (line 49) – ebb and flow, changing fortunes

---

pagan unbelieving
infidel person lacking faith
divide myself cut myself in half
go to buffets fight myself
stomach appetite
start jump, flinch

thick-eyed musing blind to everything except your own thoughts
curst melancholy bad-tempered sadness
motions expressions, twitchings
hest command
portents signs of the future

Glendower? Is there not besides the Douglas? Have I not all their
letters to meet me in arms by the ninth of the next month, and are
they not some of them set forward already? What a pagan rascal is
this, an infidel! Ha! You shall see now in very sincerity of fear and   25
cold heart will he to the King, and lay open all our proceedings! O,
I could divide myself, and go to buffets, for moving such a dish of
skim milk with so honourable an action! Hang him, let him tell the
King, we are prepared. I will set forward tonight.

Enter his LADY

How now, Kate? I must leave you within these two hours.   30
LADY PERCY O my good lord, why are you thus alone?
        For what offence have I this fortnight been
        A banished woman from my Harry's bed?
        Tell me, sweet lord, what is't that takes from thee
        Thy stomach, pleasure, and thy golden sleep?   35
        Why dost thou bend thine eyes upon the earth,
        And start so often when thou sittest alone?
        Why hast thou lost the fresh blood in thy cheeks,
        And given my treasures and my rights of thee
        To thick-eyed musing, and curst melancholy?   40
        In thy faint slumbers I by thee have watched
        And heard thee murmur tales of iron wars,
        Speak terms of manage to thy bounding steed,
        Cry 'Courage! To the field!' and thou hast talked
        Of sallies, and retires, of trenches, tents,   45
        Of palisadoes, frontiers, parapets,
        Of basilisks, of cannon, culverin,
        Of prisoners' ransom, and of soldiers slain,
        And all the currents of a heady fight.
        Thy spirit within thee hath been so at war,   50
        And thus hath so bestirred thee in thy sleep,
        That beads of sweat have stood upon thy brow
        Like bubbles in a late-disturbèd stream,
        And in thy face strange motions have appeared,
        Such as we see when men restrain their breath   55
        On some great sudden hest. O, what portents are these?
        Some heavy business hath my lord in hand,
        And I must know it, else he loves me not.

Hotspur orders his horse to be brought. His wife, suspecting a planned rebellion, continues to ask what worries Hotspur, but he refuses to give a straight answer.

1 'The packet'

Who will receive the letter that Hotspur has sent his servant Gillams to deliver (line 59)? What does the letter say? Try your hand at writing a letter in Hotspur's style.

2 Esperance! (line 65)

The motto or war cry of the Percy family was (and still is) *Esperance ma comforte* (Hope is my comfort). Design a coat of arms or shield for Hotspur which incorporates the motto.

3 'My brother Mortimer'

In lines 75–7, Kate fears (correctly) that Hotspur is about to join Mortimer and support his claim ('title') to be rightful king of England ('doth stir About his title' means 'wants to claim the throne'). She was herself a Mortimer, but in historical fact was not the sister, but great aunt, of the Edmund Mortimer who claimed the crown. For an account of Shakespeare's alteration of history, turn to page 200.

4 Servants' point of view (in pairs)

Gillams and Butler are servants who never appear in the play. What do they think of their master: his personality, his relationship with his wife, his political plans? Take parts as Gillams and Butler and improvise their conversation.

---

sheriff local magistrate
roan horse flecked with white or grey
back ride, mount
spleen hot temper
tossed with worried by
line reinforce

paraquito small parrot
mammets dolls and puppets
tilt joust like knights
crowns heads
pass them current make such fighting legal
God's me! God save me!

HOTSPUR What ho!

[*Enter a* SERVANT]

        Is Gillams with the packet gone?

SERVANT He is, my lord, an hour ago.   60

HOTSPUR Hath Butler brought those horses from the sheriff?

SERVANT One horse, my lord, he brought even now.

HOTSPUR What horse? A roan, a crop-ear is it not?

SERVANT It is, my lord.

HOTSPUR   That roan shall be my throne.

        Well, I will back him straight. O Esperance!   65

        Bid Butler lead him forth into the park.

[*Exit Servant*]

LADY PERCY But hear you, my lord.

HOTSPUR What sayest thou, my lady?

LADY PERCY What is it carries you away?

HOTSPUR Why, my horse, my love, my horse.   70

LADY PERCY Out, you mad-headed ape!

        A weasel hath not such a deal of spleen

        As you are tossed with. In faith,

        I'll know your business, Harry, that I will.

        I fear my brother Mortimer doth stir   75

        About his title, and hath sent for you

        To line his enterprise. But if you go –

HOTSPUR So far afoot I shall be weary, love.

LADY PERCY Come, come, you paraquito, answer me

        Directly unto this question that I ask.   80

        In faith, I'll break thy little finger, Harry,

        And if thou wilt not tell me all things true.

HOTSPUR Away,

        Away you trifler! Love! I love thee not,

        I care not for thee, Kate; this is no world   85

        To play with mammets, and to tilt with lips.

        We must have bloody noses, and cracked crowns,

        And pass them current too. God's me! My horse!

        What say'st thou, Kate? What wouldst thou have with me?

Lady Percy questions if Hotspur loves her, and wants to know if he is joking or not. Hotspur refuses to be questioned and implies that all women are chatterboxes. He declares he will leave tomorrow.

1 Husband and wife (in pairs)

Does Hotspur really love his wife? To explore their relationship take parts as Kate and Hotspur and speak lines 67–111. Afterwards, talk together about some or all of the following:

a Does he simply tease her, or does he mean what he says?

b Does he switch from joking to being deadly serious?

c What does Kate really think about Hotspur?

d In lines 103–6, Hotspur echoes a proverbial saying: women cannot be trusted, so the best course is not to tell them secrets. They cannot talk about what they do not know. Do you think Hotspur is joking or serious here?

e What tone of voice does Kate use at lines 107 and 111?

f How would you play the relationships on stage? What gestures, expressions, movements could help the audience understand that it is a loving or a cold relationship?

2 Women in a man's world

For activities on women in the play, see pages 124 and 184.

reason whereabout question or demand to know
Constant faithful

closer more capable of keeping a secret
of force perforce, necessarily

LADY PERCY Do you not love me? Do you not indeed?   90
     Well, do not then, for since you love me not
     I will not love myself. Do you not love me?
     Nay, tell me if you speak in jest or no?
HOTSPUR Come, wilt thou see me ride?
     And when I am a-horseback I will swear   95
     I love thee infinitely. But hark you, Kate,
     I must not have you henceforth question me
     Whither I go, nor reason whereabout.
     Whither I must, I must. And, to conclude,
     This evening must I leave you, gentle Kate.   100
     I know you wise, but yet no farther wise
     Than Harry Percy's wife. Constant you are,
     But yet a woman. And for secrecy,
     No lady closer, for I well believe
     Thou wilt not utter what thou dost not know.   105
     And so far will I trust thee, gentle Kate.
LADY PERCY How? So far?
HOTSPUR Not an inch further. But hark you, Kate,
     Whither I go, thither shall you go too.
     Today will I set forth, tomorrow you.   110
     Will this content you, Kate?
LADY PERCY   It must, of force.

Exeunt

Hal tells how he has befriended three barmen who consider him a good sport and will serve him loyally. Hal proposes that he and Poins play a trick on Francis.

1 Speak the speech!

Hal's speech paints a colourful picture of life in the Boar's Head Tavern. Three barmen ('a leash of drawers') have entertained him in the room where the barrels ('hogsheads') are kept, a place where only favourite customers are allowed.

Hal tells of drinking practices: drinking heavily is called 'dyeing scarlet' (getting a red nose); when someone pauses for breath as they drink, the other drinkers shout 'Hem!' ('Clear your throat!') and 'Play it off!' ('Drink up!'). He talks of 'tinkers' (famous for their drinking), 'bastard' (sweet Spanish wine) and 'the Half-moon' (name of a room in the inn).

Explore different ways of delivering Hal's lines opposite. Here are a few questions to help your thinking:

a Hal has been drinking. How sober is he?

b What is his attitude to the drawers: condescending, friendly, or...? How does he imitate them?

c Does he pause significantly at certain words? For example, 'humility' (line 5) as he remembers his high status; 'Tom, Dick and ...' (line 7) as he remembers his own name; 'honour' (line 17) as he speaks a key word of the play.

2 Stage design

Use Hal's language to help you design the set for this scene. As you read on, you will discover that the only necessary props are tables, chairs and a cushion.

---

fat stuffy, crowded
loggerheads blockheads
base string lowest note
upon their salvation to save their souls
Corinthian drinking partner
mettle courage

underskinker junior barman
Anon 'Coming!', 'Shortly!'
Score charge for ('put on the slate')
precedent example
Pomgarnet Pomegranate (name of room)

ACT 2 SCENE 4
Eastcheap: the Boar's Head Tavern

Enter PRINCE *and* POINS

PRINCE Ned, prithee come out of that fat room, and lend me thy hand to laugh a little.

POINS Where hast been, Hal?

PRINCE With three or four loggerheads, amongst three or fourscore hogsheads. I have sounded the very base string of humility. Sirrah, 5 I am sworn brother to a leash of drawers, and can call them all by their Christian names, as Tom, Dick, and Francis. They take it already upon their salvation that though I be but Prince of Wales yet I am the king of courtesy, and tell me flatly I am no proud Jack like Falstaff, but a Corinthian, a lad of mettle, a good boy – by the 10 Lord, so they call me! – and when I am King of England I shall command all the good lads in Eastcheap. They call drinking deep 'dyeing scarlet', and when you breathe in your watering they cry 'Hem!' and bid you 'Play it off!' To conclude, I am so good a proficient in one quarter of an hour that I can drink with any tinker 15 in his own language during my life. I tell thee, Ned, thou hast lost much honour that thou wert not with me in this action. But, sweet Ned – to sweeten which name of Ned I give thee this pennyworth of sugar, clapped even now into my hand by an underskinker, one that never spake other English in his life than 'Eight shillings and 20 sixpence', and 'You are welcome', with this shrill addition, 'Anon, anon, sir! Score a pint of bastard in the Half-moon!', or so. But Ned, to drive away the time till Falstaff come – I prithee do thou stand in some by-room while I question my puny drawer to what end he gave me the sugar. And do thou never leave calling 'Francis!', that 25 his tale to me may be nothing but 'Anon'. Step aside, and I'll show thee a precedent.

[Poins withdraws]

POINS *[Within]* Francis!

PRINCE Thou art perfect.

POINS *[Within]* Francis! 30

Enter FRANCIS, *a Drawer*

FRANCIS Anon, anon, sir. Look down into the Pomgarnet, Ralph!

Hal questions Francis, who tries to reply but is distracted by Poins calling for him from the next room. Hal talks increasing gibberish and Francis is totally confused.

1 Who is the fool? (in groups of three)

As Hal questions Francis, Poins calls for service. Francis is torn between replying to the Prince (who seems to be offering him a job or a large amount of money), and going off to serve Poins.

Hal deliberately confuses Francis in lines 56–66, talking greater and greater nonsense. Explanations of his words are given below and at the foot of the page. But it probably isn't worthwhile trying to make precise sense out of what Hal says. The general impression is that he seems to imply that Francis had best stick to his job of waiting on customers (lines 64–6), and that he gives a picture of an innkeeper:

'not-pated' (line 60) – short-haired

'puke' (line 61) – blue-grey wool

'caddis' (line 61) – woollen ribbons

'smooth-tongue' (line 61) – flattering, fast talking

In the theatre, actors usually try to make this episode as funny as possible. But there are other ways of playing or thinking about the scene. Give your response to what one student wrote:

'This is a mean-spirited joke. It is the kind of thing that upper-class twits think is funny, taking the mickey out of servants. It shows that Hal doesn't have much intelligence or a real sense of humour (as Poins implies at line 80). I'd like to see it played on stage in a way that shows up Hal as stupid, rather than Francis. Hal is unfairly using his position as a Prince to humiliate.'

How would you want the audience to respond if you were directing the play? Take parts and present your own version of lines 28–69.

---

serve complete your apprenticeship
By'r lady By the Virgin Mary
clinking of pewter serving tankards of ale
indenture contract of apprenticeship

books bibles
Michaelmas 29 September
Spanish pouch leather moneybag from Spain
sully become dirty
Barbary North Africa

PRINCE Come hither, Francis.

FRANCIS My lord?

PRINCE How long hast thou to serve, Francis?

FRANCIS Forsooth, five years, and as much as to –   35

POINS [*Within*] Francis!

FRANCIS Anon, anon, sir.

PRINCE Five year! By'r lady, a long lease for the clinking of pewter. But
Francis, darest thou be so valiant as to play the coward with thy
indenture, and show it a fair pair of heels, and run from it?   40

FRANCIS O Lord, sir, I'll be sworn upon all the books in England, I
could find in my heart –

POINS [*Within*] Francis!

FRANCIS Anon, sir.

PRINCE How old art thou, Francis?   45

FRANCIS Let me see, about Michaelmas next I shall be –

POINS [*Within*] Francis!

FRANCIS Anon, sir – pray stay a little, my lord.

PRINCE Nay but hark you, Francis, for the sugar thou gavest me, 'twas
a pennyworth, was't not?   50

FRANCIS O Lord, I would it had been two!

PRINCE I will give thee for it a thousand pound – ask me when thou wilt,
and thou shalt have it.

POINS [*Within*] Francis!

FRANCIS Anon, anon.   55

PRINCE Anon, Francis? No, Francis, but tomorrow, Francis. Or
Francis, a-Thursday. Or indeed Francis, when thou wilt. But
Francis!

FRANCIS My lord?

PRINCE Wilt thou rob this leathern-jerkin, crystal-button, not-pated,   60
agate-ring, puke-stocking, caddis-garter, smooth-tongue Spanish
pouch?

FRANCIS O Lord, sir, who do you mean?

PRINCE Why then your brown bastard is your only drink. For look you,
Francis, your white canvas doublet will sully. In Barbary, sir, it   65
cannot come to so much.

FRANCIS What, sir?

POINS [*Within*] Francis!

PRINCE Away, you rogue, dost thou not hear them call?
*Here they both call him; the Drawer stands amazed,
not knowing which way to go*

63

Falstaff waits outside the room. Poins asks Hal what the trick on Francis was all about. Hal replies he is in a mood for anything, and imitates Hotspur. He orders Falstaff be admitted.

1 Design the Vintner's costume

The Vintner is the landlord of the tavern. Only a few lines earlier Hal described such a London innkeeper. Use lines 60–2 to help you design a costume for the Vintner.

2 Puzzles about the Prince

Hal is Prince of Wales, the highest status person in England after his father, King Henry. This scene raises a number of puzzles about his personality and relationships:

a Why does Hal keep Falstaff waiting outside, rather than inviting him in straightaway?

b Poins calls Hal 'my lad' at line 79. How does Hal react to such a familiar expression?

c Poins is puzzled by the joke played on Francis. Hal does not answer his question at line 80. Many critics have explained the trick as a part of Prince Hal's education, as he learns about the low-status people of England. How convincing do you find such an explanation?

d Why does Hal suddenly speak of Hotspur?

e Speak Hal's lines 91–4, which imitate Hotspur. How well do you think Hal has captured Hotspur's style? Briefly suggest three or four ways in which Hal is different from Hotspur.

---

crickets chirruping insects
cunning match clever point
humours moods
goodman Adam yeoman Adam (in the Bible, the first man)
pupil age youthfulness

parcel of a reckoning adding up of a bill
drench dose of medicine
brawn boars' meat (Falstaff)
Rivo! Cheers!
Ribs ... Tallow meat, fat

Enter VINTNER

VINTNER What, standest thou still and hearest such a calling? Look to   70
the guests within.

[*Exit Francis*]

My lord, old Sir John with half-a-dozen more are at the door. Shall
I let them in?

PRINCE Let them alone a while, and then open the door.

[*Exit Vintner*]

Enter POINS

Poins!   75

POINS Anon, anon, sir.

PRINCE Sirrah, Falstaff and the rest of the thieves are at the door. Shall
we be merry?

POINS As merry as crickets, my lad. But hark ye, what cunning match
have you made with this jest of the drawer? Come, what's the issue?   80

PRINCE I am now of all humours that have showed themselves humours
since the old days of goodman Adam to the pupil age of this present
twelve o'clock at midnight.

[*Enter* FRANCIS]

What's o'clock, Francis?

FRANCIS Anon, anon, sir.   [*Exit*]   85

PRINCE That ever this fellow should have fewer words than a parrot,
and yet the son of a woman! His industry is up-stairs and down-
stairs, his eloquence the parcel of a reckoning. I am not yet of
Percy's mind, the Hotspur of the north, he that kills me some six
or seven dozen of Scots at a breakfast, washes his hands, and says   90
to his wife, 'Fie upon this quiet life, I want work.' 'O my sweet
Harry', says she, 'how many hast thou killed today?' 'Give my roan
horse a drench', says he, and answers, 'Some fourteen', an hour
after, 'a trifle, a trifle'. I prithee, call in Falstaff. I'll play Percy, and
that damned brawn shall play Dame Mortimer his wife. 'Rivo!'   95
says the drunkard. Call in Ribs, call in Tallow!

Enter FALSTAFF [, GADSHILL, BARDOLPH, *and* PETO;
followed by FRANCIS, *with wine*]

POINS Welcome, Jack, where hast thou been?

Falstaff expresses contempt for all cowards. He complains that his wine is bitter and that England is going to the dogs. He jeers at Hal and Poins and boasts of a rich robbery.

1 Falstaff tells his tale (in groups of four or more)

In Act 1 Scene 2, lines 148–51, Poins predicted that Falstaff would invent incredible lies to explain away the robbery at Gad's Hill. Sure enough, that is just what Falstaff will now do throughout lines 98–233.

Take parts as Falstaff, Hal, Poins and a director who can also speak as Peto and Bardolph. First speak the lines, then rehearse a performance.

2 Titan melts the butter

Hal's lines 102–4 have puzzled many people. 'Titan' is the sun, and the general sense seems to be that Falstaff, drinking his wine, is like the sun melting a dish of butter. Should Hal point emphatically at Falstaff as he says 'behold that compound'?

3 Weavers

Falstaff often pretends to be virtuous and religious. Weavers (line 112) were known for their puritanism and psalm singing. But how does Falstaff speak 'or anything'? Does he have very different (vulgar) songs in his mind?

4 Cowards

Falstaff talks incessantly of cowards. But the question whether he himself is a coward runs through the play. At lines 123–8 the actor playing Falstaff can choose whether or not to display cowardice when he responds to Poins' threat to stab him. How do you think Falstaff should speak the lines?

---

nether-stocks stockings	**woolsack** huge bale of wool
extant living	**dagger of lath** wooden dagger
lime used to make wine less sweet	used by the character Vice in
shotten herring skinny fish	medieval morality plays

FALSTAFF A plague of all cowards, I say, and a vengeance too, marry
and amen! Give me a cup of sack, boy. Ere I lead this life long, I'll
sew nether-stocks, and mend them and foot them too. A plague of   100
all cowards! Give me a cup of sack, rogue. Is there no virtue extant?
He drinks

PRINCE Didst thou never see Titan kiss a dish of butter – pitiful-
hearted Titan! – that melted at the sweet tale of the sun's? If thou
didst, then behold that compound.

FALSTAFF You rogue, here's lime in this sack too. There is nothing but   105
roguery to be found in villainous man, yet a coward is worse than
a cup of sack with lime in it. A villainous coward! Go thy ways, old
Jack, die when thou wilt. If manhood, good manhood, be not forgot
upon the face of the earth, then am I a shotten herring. There lives
not three good men unhanged in England, and one of them is fat,   110
and grows old. God help the while, a bad world I say. I would I
were a weaver: I could sing psalms – or anything. A plague of all
cowards, I say still.

PRINCE How now, woolsack, what mutter you?

FALSTAFF A king's son! If I do not beat thee out of thy kingdom with a   115
dagger of lath, and drive all thy subjects afore thee like a flock of
wild geese, I'll never wear hair on my face more. You, Prince of
Wales!

PRINCE Why, you whoreson round man, what's the matter?

FALSTAFF Are not you a coward? Answer me to that – and Poins there?   120

POINS Zounds, ye fat paunch, an ye call me coward by the Lord I'll stab
thee.

FALSTAFF I call thee coward? I'll see thee damned ere I call thee coward,
but I would give a thousand pound I could run as fast as thou canst.
You are straight enough in the shoulders, you care not who sees   125
your back. Call you that backing of your friends? A plague upon
such backing, give me them that will face me! Give me a cup of
sack! I am a rogue if I drunk today.

PRINCE O, villain! Thy lips are scarce wiped since thou drunk'st last.

FALSTAFF All is one for that. (*He drinks.*) A plague of all cowards, still   130
say I.

PRINCE What's the matter?

FALSTAFF What's the matter? There be four of us here have taken a
thousand pound this day morning.

PRINCE Where is it, Jack, where is it?   135

Falstaff tells his story, accompanying his lies with demonstrations of his sword-fighting skills. Each time he speaks, he increases the number of men he fought.

'*ecce signum!*' (behold the sign!). Falstaff produces the evidence.

1 Active story-telling

Falstaff's story is full of implicit stage directions. Here are a few examples of where Falstaff can physically demonstrate what he says:

lines 142–3 '*ecce signum!*' see illustration above

line 161 'I have peppered two of them' (filled them full of holes?)

line 164 'my old ward' (my famous sword-fencing posture)

line 164 'here I lay, and thus I bore my point' (here I struck, and here's how I held my sword)

line 174 'by these hilts' (holds up a sword-hilt like a cross)

---

half-sword hand-to-hand fighting
doublet, hose jacket, stockings
buckler small round shield
All would not do no one could
 do better

Ebrew Jew a proper Jew
paid killed
target small shield

FALSTAFF Where is it? Taken from us it is. A hundred upon poor four
of us.

PRINCE What, a hundred, man?

FALSTAFF I am a rogue if I were not at half-sword with a dozen of them
two hours together. I have scaped by miracle. I am eight times   140
thrust through the doublet, four through the hose, my buckler cut
through and through, my sword hacked like a handsaw – *ecce
signum*! I never dealt better since I was a man. All would not do. A
plague of all cowards! Let them speak. If they speak more or less
than truth, they are villains and the sons of darkness.   145

[PRINCE] Speak, sirs, how was it?

[BARDOLPH] We four set upon some dozen –

FALSTAFF Sixteen at least, my lord.

[BARDOLPH] And bound them.

PETO No, no, they were not bound.   150

FALSTAFF You rogue, they were bound, every man of them, or I am a
Jew else: an Ebrew Jew.

[BARDOLPH] As we were sharing, some six or seven fresh men set upon
us –

FALSTAFF And unbound the rest, and then come in the other.   155

PRINCE What, fought you with them all?

FALSTAFF All? I know not what you call all, but if I fought not with fifty
of them I am a bunch of radish. If there were not two or three and
fifty upon poor old Jack, then am I no two-legg'd creature.

PRINCE Pray God you have not murdered some of them.   160

FALSTAFF Nay, that's past praying for, I have peppered two of them.
Two I am sure I have paid, two rogues in buckram suits. I tell thee
what, Hal, if I tell thee a lie, spit in my face, call me horse. Thou
knowest my old ward – here I lay, and thus I bore my point. Four
rogues in buckram let drive at me –   165

PRINCE What, four? Thou saidst but two even now.

FALSTAFF Four, Hal, I told thee four.

POINS Ay, ay, he said four.

FALSTAFF These four came all afront, and mainly thrust at me. I made
me no more ado, but took all their seven points in my target, thus!   170

PRINCE Seven? Why, there were but four even now.

FALSTAFF In buckram?

POINS Aye, four, in buckram suits.

FALSTAFF Seven, by these hilts, or I am a villain else.

PRINCE Prithee let him alone, we shall have more anon.   175

Falstaff continues to elaborate his story, but Hal catches him out: if it were dark, Falstaff could not see colours. Falstaff refuses to explain, and he and Hal exchange insults.

1 Lost puns?

Some of Shakespeare's verbal humour is unfamiliar to a modern audience because of changes in meaning or pronunciation.

- Poins puns on 'points' at lines 181–2. Falstaff means 'the points of their swords', but an Elizabethan man's 'points' were also the laces that held up his stockings ('hose').
- Falstaff loves to pun. In Shakespeare's time, 'reasons' was pronounced 'raisins', which probably caused a laughter among the Elizabethan audience at line 199.

Suggest ways in which the actors might help a modern audience to understand and enjoy the puns.

2 Insults (in pairs or groups)

Take parts and speak the insults Hal and Falstaff exchange at lines 190–1 and 201–6. Invent gestures to accompany each insult. What do the insults suggest about the actual physical appearance of the two men? For example, a 'tailor's-yard' is a yardstick for measuring cloth, and a 'bow-case' is a narrow bag for a longbow.

3 Does Falstaff know?

Does Falstaff know all along that he was robbed by Hal and Poins? Is he deliberately making himself appear ridiculous for the entertainment of Hal? Keep these questions in mind as you continue to build up your impression of Falstaff's character.

---

give me ground retreat from me
tallow-catch pan to catch fat from roasting meat
at the strappado, or all the racks being tortured by hanging or stretching

sanguine courageous
elf-skin skin of an elf or eel
neat's-tongue ox's tongue
pizzle penis
stock-fish dried cod
standing tuck upright rapier

FALSTAFF Dost thou hear me, Hal?

PRINCE Ay, and mark thee too, Jack.

FALSTAFF Do so, for it is worth the listening to. These nine in buckram
that I told thee of –

PRINCE So, two more already. 180

FALSTAFF Their points being broken –

POINS Down fell their hose.

FALSTAFF – began to give me ground. But I followed me close, came in,
foot and hand, and, with a thought, seven of the eleven I paid.

PRINCE O monstrous! Eleven buckram men grown out of two! 185

FALSTAFF But as the devil would have it, three misbegotten knaves in
Kendal green came at my back and let drive at me, for it was so
dark, Hal, that thou couldst not see thy hand.

PRINCE These lies are like their father that begets them, gross as a
mountain, open, palpable. Why, thou clay-brained guts, thou 190
knotty-pated fool, thou whoreson obscene greasy tallow-catch –

FALSTAFF What, art thou mad? Art thou mad? Is not the truth the truth?

PRINCE Why, how couldst thou know these men in Kendal green when
it was so dark thou couldst not see thy hand? Come, tell us your
reason. What sayest thou to this? 195

POINS Come, your reason, Jack, your reason!

FALSTAFF What, upon compulsion? Zounds, an I were at the strappado,
or all the racks in the world, I would not tell you on compulsion.
Give you a reason on compulsion? If reasons were as plentiful as
blackberries, I would give no man a reason upon compulsion, I. 200

PRINCE I'll be no longer guilty of this sin. This sanguine coward, this
bed-presser, this horse-back-breaker, this huge hill of flesh –

FALSTAFF 'Sblood, you starveling, you elf-skin, you dried neat's-tongue,
you bull's-pizzle, you stock-fish! O for breath to utter what is like
thee! You tailor's-yard, you sheath, you bow-case, you vile standing 205
tuck!

PRINCE Well, breathe a while, and then to it again, and when thou hast
tired thyself in base comparisons hear me speak but this.

POINS Mark, Jack!

Hal recounts what really happened at Gad's Hill. Falstaff says that he knew all along that it was Hal, and that his natural instinct explains his behaviour. A messenger arrives from the king.

1 Get out of that!

Hal and Poins challenge Falstaff to invent some explanation for his cowardly behaviour at Gad's Hill. Falstaff's reply (lines 221–31) is a series of short sentences. The actor's task is to make them as funny as possible in their truthfulness or untruthfulness.

a How long a pause before Falstaff begins his explanation at line 221? Should the actor show Falstaff desperately seeking for a long while in his mind for some possible excuse?

b Find a suitable tone for Falstaff to speak 'I knew ye as well as he that made ye'. Is it with self-satisfied humour, patronising Hal for his foolishness, or in some other way?

c 'instinct': Falstaff appeals to instinct: his natural intuition that a Prince must always be respected. Try to speak the lines as if Falstaff knows that it is an evident lie, but its humour will keep him good friends with Hal.

2 Hal's humour

Hal's reply to the news that a nobleman has arrived at the door is obscure to most members of a modern audience, but for Elizabethans it was a popular joke about money. A noble was worth one third of £1 sterling; a royal worth half of £1.

Do you think Hal's mention of his mother has any significance other than as a humorous contrast to 'father'?

---

out-faced detached	**clap to** slam, lock
device deceit	**Watch** revel
starting-hole hiding place	**extempore** improvised, impromptu
Hercules (in Classical mythology)	**argument** plot
a superhuman hero	**gravity** a respectable old man

PRINCE We two saw you four set on four, and bound them and were 210
masters of their wealth – mark now how a plain tale shall put you
down. Then did we two set on you four, and, with a word, out-
faced you from your prize, and have it, yea, and can show it you
here in the house. And Falstaff, you carried your guts away as
nimbly, with as quick dexterity, and roared for mercy, and still run 215
and roared, as ever I heard bull-calf. What a slave art thou to hack
thy sword as thou hast done, and then say it was in fight! What
trick, what device, what starting-hole canst thou now find out, to
hide thee from this open and apparent shame?

POINS Come, let's hear Jack, what trick hast thou now? 220

FALSTAFF By the Lord, I knew ye as well as he that made ye. Why, hear
you, my masters, was it for me to kill the heir apparent? Should I
turn upon the true prince? Why, thou knowest I am as valiant as
Hercules. But beware instinct. The lion will not touch the true
prince. Instinct is a great matter. I was now a coward on instinct. I 225
shall think the better of myself, and thee, during my life – I for a
valiant lion, and thou for a true prince. But by the Lord, lads, I am
glad you have the money! Hostess, clap to the doors! Watch
tonight, pray tomorrow! Gallants, lads, boys, hearts of gold, all the
titles of good fellowship come to you! What, shall we be merry? 230
Shall we have a play extempore?

PRINCE Content, and the argument shall be thy running away.

FALSTAFF Ah, no more of that Hal, an thou lovest me.

Enter HOSTESS

HOSTESS O Jesu, my lord the Prince!

PRINCE How now, my lady the Hostess, what sayest thou to me? 235

HOSTESS Marry my lord, there is a nobleman of the court at door would
speak with you. He says he comes from your father.

PRINCE Give him as much as will make him a royal man and send him
back again to my mother.

FALSTAFF What manner of man is he? 240

HOSTESS An old man.

FALSTAFF What doth gravity out of his bed at midnight? Shall I give
him his answer?

PRINCE Prithee do, Jack.

FALSTAFF Faith, and I'll send him packing. *Exit* 245

*Peto and Bardolph explain that Falstaff invented all the signs of a
bloody fight in order to excuse their running away. Falstaff brings news
of stirrings of rebellion by Hotspur and Glendower.*

1 What is Bardolph like?

Bardolph claims that he was so ashamed at obeying Falstaff and
pretending to be injured in a fight, that he blushed for the first time in
seven years. Hal replies that Bardolph's red face is caused by hard
drinking.

What does Bardolph look like? He calls the boils and pimples on his
face 'meteors' and 'exhalations' (shooting stars). But he claims that
they show his true nature, not a drunkard but a soldier full of anger
('choler'). Hal puns on 'choler' and 'collar' saying that they show
Bardolph's future is to be hanged: a 'halter' is a hangman's noose (or
collar). It is an ominous prediction, because in *King Henry V*, shortly
before the battle of Agincourt, Hal (now King) orders Bardolph's
execution for theft.

Use lines 259–69 to invent Bardolph's life story. How did he come
to be a companion of Falstaff? See also Act 3 Scene 3, lines 22–37.

2 Hints of Glendower

When Glendower appears (Act 3 Scene 1) it becomes clear why
Falstaff describes him in such extravagant terms in lines 278–81.
Falstaff gives him magical supernatural powers. He is able to punish
devils by beating the soles of their feet ('the bastinado'). He seduced
the wife of the king of the devils ('made Lucifer cuckold') and so gave
the Devil his horns (cuckolds were deceived husbands, and were
believed to have horns). He even made the Devil his faithful follower
by forcing him to swear an oath on a Welsh hook (a farmer's billhook).
Keep Falstaff's description in mind and compare it with Glendower as
revealed in the next scene.

---

spear-grass sharp-edged grass
beslubber smear
devices deceits
taken with the manner caught
  red-handed
extempore spontaneously

Hot livers, and cold purses
  drunken courage and no money
creature of bombast braggart,
  wearer of over-padded clothes
Amamon a devil

PRINCE Now sirs, by'r lady, you fought fair, so did you, Peto, so did you, Bardolph. You are lions too, you ran away upon instinct, you will not touch the true prince, no, fie!

BARDOLPH Faith, I ran when I saw others run.

PRINCE Faith, tell me now in earnest, how came Falstaff's sword so   250
hacked?

PETO Why, he hacked it with his dagger, and said he would swear truth out of England but he would make you believe it was done in fight, and persuaded us to do the like.

BARDOLPH Yea, and to tickle our noses with spear-grass, to make them   255
bleed, and then to beslubber our garments with it, and swear it was the blood of true men. I did that I did not this seven year before: I blushed to hear his monstrous devices.

PRINCE O villain, thou stolest a cup of sack eighteen years ago, and wert taken with the manner, and ever since thou hast blushed extempore.   260
Thou hadst fire and sword on thy side, and yet thou ran'st away. What instinct hadst thou for it?

BARDOLPH My lord, do you see these meteors? Do you behold these exhalations?

PRINCE I do.   265

BARDOLPH What think you they portend?

PRINCE Hot livers, and cold purses.

BARDOLPH Choler, my lord, if rightly taken.

PRINCE No, if rightly taken, halter.

Enter FALSTAFF

Here comes lean Jack, here comes bare-bone. How now my sweet   270
creature of bombast, how long is't ago, Jack, since thou sawest thine own knee?

FALSTAFF My own knee? When I was about thy years, Hal, I was not an eagle's talon in the waist – I could have crept into any alderman's thumb-ring. A plague of sighing and grief, it blows a man up like   275
a bladder. There's villainous news abroad. Here was Sir John Bracy from your father. You must to the court in the morning. That same mad fellow of the north, Percy, and he of Wales that gave Amamon the bastinado, and made Lucifer cuckold, and swore the devil his true liegeman upon the cross of a Welsh hook – what   280
a plague call you him?

POINS O, Glendower.

75

Falstaff announces that Northumberland and the Scots and Welsh are gathering, and that civil war threatens. Hal denies he is afraid. Falstaff warns Hal to prepare to face his father, King Henry.

1 The joke's over?

Hal continues to taunt Falstaff with cowardice in running away. Falstaff first calls him 'cuckoo' (line 292) because of the repetitive call of that bird.

When Hal once again reminds him of instinct, Falstaff replies 'I grant ye, upon instinct' (line 294). In what tone of voice do you think Falstaff speaks these five words?

2 Male humour: funny or brutal?

Hal jokes that in a civil war, women become easily available (lines 298–300). Do you think Hal is simply joking, or might he be serious? Think about your own response to his lines, then step into role as director of the play. Decide how would you want the audience to respond, and what advice you would give to the actor to help him evoke that response.

3 'King Cambyses' vein'

Falstaff is about to play Hal's father, to question Hal about his behaviour. He says he will play the part of King Henry 'in King Cambyses' vein': a melodramatic ranting manner. *Cambyses King of Persia* was a play written in 1569. Its high-flown, extravagant style is parodied in *A Midsummer Night's Dream* in the Mechanicals' play of Pyramus and Thisbe.

Turn the page to find how Falstaff delivers his own parody of such bombastic style.

---

blue-caps Scottish soldiers
stinking mackerel rotten fish
civil buffeting civil war
hob-nails heavy nails for boots

chid criticised
joint-stool wooden stool
here is my leg I'll make a bow

FALSTAFF Owen, Owen, the same. And his son-in-law Mortimer, and old Northumberland, and that sprightly Scot of Scots, Douglas, that runs a-horseback up a hill perpendicular – 285

PRINCE He that rides at high speed, and with his pistol kills a sparrow flying.

FALSTAFF You have hit it.

PRINCE So did he never the sparrow.

FALSTAFF Well, that rascal hath good mettle in him, he will not run. 290

PRINCE Why, what a rascal art thou then, to praise him so for running!

FALSTAFF A-horseback, ye cuckoo, but afoot he will not budge a foot.

PRINCE Yes, Jack, upon instinct.

FALSTAFF I grant ye, upon instinct. Well, he is there too, and one Mordake, and a thousand blue-caps more. Worcester is stolen 295 away tonight. Thy father's beard is turned white with the news. You may buy land now as cheap as stinking mackerel.

PRINCE Why then, it is like if there come a hot June, and this civil buffeting hold, we shall buy maidenheads as they buy hob-nails, by the hundreds. 300

FALSTAFF By the mass, lad, thou sayest true, it is like we shall have good trading that way. But tell me, Hal, art not thou horrible afeard? Thou being heir apparent, could the world pick thee out three such enemies again, as that fiend Douglas, that spirit Percy, and that devil Glendower? Art thou not horribly afraid? Doth not thy blood 305 thrill at it?

PRINCE Not a whit, i'faith, I lack some of thy instinct.

FALSTAFF Well, thou wilt be horribly chid tomorrow when thou comest to thy father. If thou love me, practise an answer.

PRINCE Do thou stand for my father and examine me upon the particu- 310 lars of my life.

FALSTAFF Shall I? Content! This chair shall be my state, this dagger my sceptre, and this cushion my crown.

PRINCE Thy state is taken for a joint-stool, thy golden sceptre for a leaden dagger, and thy precious rich crown for a pitiful bald crown. 315

FALSTAFF Well, an the fire of grace be not quite out of thee, now shalt thou be moved. Give me a cup of sack to make my eyes look red, that it may be thought I have wept, for I must speak in passion, and I will do it in King Cambyses' vein.

PRINCE Well, here is my leg. 320

FALSTAFF And here is my speech. Stand aside, nobility.

HOSTESS O Jesu, this is excellent sport, i'faith.

Falstaff mockingly acts the role of King Henry, joking at Hal's expense, warning him about keeping bad company, but praising Falstaff. Hal decides to play the king himself.

1 Act it out (in groups of three)

Falstaff adopts a high-flown, affected style. He pretends to be very wise, and often uses a moralistic tone, like an old-fashioned Puritan preacher. His language is a parody of many kinds of speech and writing: old morality plays, the Bible, and everyday proverbs. It also parodies the Elizabethan writer John Lyly who used very flowery, elaborate language in his prose narrative *Euphues*.

Take parts as Falstaff, Hal and the Hostess (who can also direct). Act out their improvised play (lines 310–99). Look out for opportunities to heighten the comedy through:

- the wordy, pretentious language that mocks old plays for example, 'convey' (take away), 'tristful' (sad) 'floodgates of her eyes' (weeping queens occurred frequently in old plays).

- echoes of the Bible: 'pitch' (line 341) is a black sticky substance. A line in the Bible says 'He that touches pitch shall be defiled'.

- very rhythmical style: using repetition, balanced sentences, rhetorical questions.

- use of comparisons from nature to teach a moral. Camomile (lines 331–3) is a flower which grows from being stepped on. See also 'fruit/tree' (line 353).

- Falstaff's humour contains uncomfortable truths. Hal is keeping dubious company, he is 'pointed at' (gossiped about), he has taken part in a robbery. When Falstaff says 'Depose me?' his words are a reminder that Henry IV deposed the rightful King Richard II and seized the throne.

---

holds his countenance keeps a straight face
harlotry players disreputable actors
nether lower
warrant me confirm my belief
micher truant (moocher)
portly stately

a corpulent well-built
three score sixty
lewdly given over-sexed and wicked
rabbit-sucker baby rabbit
poulter's hare hare hanging in poultry-seller's window

FALSTAFF Weep not, sweet Queen, for trickling tears are vain.

HOSTESS O the Father, how he holds his countenance!

FALSTAFF For God's sake, lords, convey my tristful Queen, 325
    For tears do stop the floodgates of her eyes.

HOSTESS O Jesu, he doth it as like one of these harlotry players as ever
I see!

FALSTAFF Peace, good pint-pot, peace, good tickle-brain. Harry, I do
not only marvel where thou spendest thy time, but also how thou 330
art accompanied. For though the camomile, the more it is trodden
on the faster it grows, yet youth, the more it is wasted the sooner it
wears. That thou art my son I have partly thy mother's word,
partly my own opinion, but chiefly a villainous trick of thine eye,
and a foolish hanging of thy nether lip, that doth warrant me. If 335
then thou be son to me – here lies the point – why, being son to me,
art thou so pointed at? Shall the blessed sun of heaven prove a
micher, and eat blackberries? A question not to be asked. Shall the
son of England prove a thief, and take purses? A question to be
asked. There is a thing, Harry, which thou hast often heard of, and 340
it is known to many in our land by the name of pitch. This pitch –
as ancient writers do report – doth defile, so doth the company thou
keepest. For, Harry, now I do not speak to thee in drink, but in
tears; not in pleasure, but in passion; not in words only, but in woes
also. And yet there is a virtuous man whom I have often noted in 345
thy company, but I know not his name.

PRINCE What manner of man, an it like your majesty?

FALSTAFF A goodly portly man, i'faith, and a corpulent; of a cheerful
look, a pleasing eye, and a most noble carriage; and, as I think, his
age some fifty, or by'r lady, inclining to three score. And now I 350
remember me, his name is Falstaff. If that man should be lewdly
given, he deceiveth me, for, Harry, I see virtue in his looks. If then
the tree may be known by the fruit, as the fruit by the tree, then
peremptorily I speak it, there is virtue in that Falstaff. Him keep
with, the rest banish. And tell me now, thou naughty varlet, tell me 355
where hast thou been this month?

PRINCE Dost thou speak like a king? Do thou stand for me, and I'll play
my father.

FALSTAFF Depose me? If thou dost it half so gravely, so majestically,
both in word and matter, hang me up by the heels for a rabbit- 360
sucker, or a poulter's hare.

*Hal, playing King Henry, delivers a damning condemnation of Falstaff.
Falstaff (as Hal) defends himself and pleads for all the tavern crew to be
banished except himself. Hal predicts Falstaff's banishment.*

1 Act it out (continued from page 78)

Use the following to help your rehearsal of the episode:

- How 'serious' are Hal and Falstaff? Do they use the roles they are playing to speak what they truly feel?
- Line 362: just where is Hal 'set'? Does he sit in the same chair and use the same props as Falstaff?
- Lines 367–8: 'I'll tickle ye ...' (I'll make you laugh). Is this an aside to the audience? or to Hal? or ...?
- Line 375: Manningtree, a town in Essex, was known for its ox-roasting festivities at which plays were sometimes performed.
- Line 376: Vice, Iniquity, Ruffian and Vanity were all characters in medieval morality plays. The role of Vice was to corrupt young men and women (in line 383, Hal calls Falstaff a 'villainous abominable misleader of youth').
- Line 381: what tone does Falstaff use to ask Hal who he is describing?
- Lines 393–8: is Falstaff's plea for everyone to be banished except himself spoken humorously, or in desperation, or ...? Does he think that Hal will banish him?
- Line 399: 'I do, I will'. This is a key line that every modern production identifies as an intensely dramatic moment in the play. How does Hal speak? How does Falstaff respond?

tun large barrel, ton
trunk of humours body full of moods
bolting-hutch waste bin
dropsies diseases
bombard leather wine bottle
cloak-bag large hold-all

neat and cleanly skilful
whoremaster pimp
Pharaoh's lean kine in the Bible, Pharaoh dreams of seven lean cows eating seven fat ones: a prediction of seven years of famine

PRINCE Well, here I am set.

FALSTAFF And here I stand. Judge, my masters.

PRINCE Now, Harry, whence come you?

FALSTAFF My noble lord, from Eastcheap.   365

PRINCE The complaints I hear of thee are grievous.

FALSTAFF 'Sblood, my lord, they are false! Nay, I'll tickle ye for a young
     prince, i'faith.

PRINCE Swearest thou, ungracious boy? Henceforth ne'er look on me.
     Thou art violently carried away from grace. There is a devil haunts   370
     thee in the likeness of an old fat man, a tun of man is thy
     companion. Why dost thou converse with that trunk of humours,
     that bolting-hutch of beastliness, that swollen parcel of dropsies,
     that huge bombard of sack, that stuffed cloak-bag of guts, that
     roasted Manningtree ox with the pudding in his belly, that reverend   375
     Vice, that grey Iniquity, that Father Ruffian, that Vanity in years?
     Wherein is he good, but to taste sack and drink it? Wherein neat
     and cleanly, but to carve a capon and eat it? Wherein cunning, but
     in craft? Wherein crafty, but in villainy? Wherein villainous, but in
     all things? Wherein worthy, but in nothing?   380

FALSTAFF I would your grace would take me with you. Whom means
     your grace?

PRINCE That villainous abominable misleader of youth, Falstaff, that
     old white-bearded Satan.

FALSTAFF My lord, the man I know.   385

PRINCE I know thou dost.

FALSTAFF But to say I know more harm in him than in myself were to
     say more than I know. That he is old, the more the pity, his white
     hairs do witness it, but that he is, saving your reverence, a
     whoremaster, that I utterly deny. If sack and sugar be a fault, God   390
     help the wicked! If to be old and merry be a sin, then many an old
     host that I know is damned. If to be fat be to be hated, then
     Pharaoh's lean kine are to be loved. No, my good lord! Banish Peto,
     banish Bardolph, banish Poins – but for sweet Jack Falstaff, kind
     Jack Falstaff, true Jack Falstaff, valiant Jack Falstaff – and therefore   395
     more valiant, being as he is old Jack Falstaff – banish not him thy
     Harry's company, banish not him thy Harry's company. Banish
     plump Jack, and banish all the world.

PRINCE I do, I will.

                        [*A knocking heard*]
                    [*Exeunt Hostess, Francis, and Bardolph*]

The Sheriff is about to enter. Falstaff asks Hal to protect him, but says he will accept death bravely. Falstaff hides behind the curtain. The Sheriff reports he has followed thieves to the tavern.

1 'Therefore I'll hide me'

Invent an exit for Falstaff that you think expresses his character. Does he make a cowardly and hasty, or a brave and dignified, exit?

2 Help with language

a Falstaff's lines 409–10 have puzzled scholars for hundreds of years. One possible interpretation is that just as a genuine coin should not be called a fraud, so too Hal, although he appears to be a rogue and idler, is in fact an honest, true man. But might the lines be about Falstaff himself? Suggest your own interpretation.

b 'The devil rides upon a fiddle-stick'. Hal's expression in line 405 has been interpreted in many ways: from 'All hell's broken loose' to 'this is much ado about nothing'. Make your own suggestion.

c When Falstaff says 'I deny your major' (line 412) he is using a technical term from philosophical debate. It means to deny the major premise (basic assumption) of your opponent's argument. What assumption of Hal's is Falstaff denying here?

d 'A hue and cry' (line 422). Right up to the nineteenth century, a hue and cry was a popular way of pursuing and capturing wrongdoers. A group of people would follow a thief, making as much noise as they could, until they had trapped and arrested the criminal.

---

most monstrous watch large troop of citizens
become not a cart don't look brave in a hangman's cart going to the gallows

arras curtain dividing off part of room
date is out 'sell-by' date has passed

Enter BARDOLPH *running*

BARDOLPH O my lord, my lord, the Sheriff with a most monstrous   400
  watch is at the door.
FALSTAFF Out, ye rogue! Play out the play! I have much to say in the
  behalf of that Falstaff.

Enter the HOSTESS

HOSTESS O Jesu, my lord, my lord!
PRINCE Heigh, heigh, the devil rides upon a fiddle-stick. What's the   405
  matter?
HOSTESS The Sheriff and all the watch are at the door. They are come
  to search the house. Shall I let them in?
FALSTAFF Dost thou hear, Hal? Never call a true piece of gold a
  counterfeit. Thou art essentially made without seeming so.   410
PRINCE And thou a natural coward without instinct.
FALSTAFF I deny your major. If you will deny the Sheriff, so; if not, let
  him enter. If I become not a cart as well as another man, a plague
  on my bringing up! I hope I shall as soon be strangled with a halter
  as another.   415
PRINCE Go hide thee behind the arras, the rest walk up above. Now, my
  masters, for a true face, and good conscience.
FALSTAFF Both which I have had, but their date is out, and therefore I'll
  hide me.

[*Exeunt all but the Prince and Peto*]

PRINCE Call in the Sheriff.   420

Enter SHERIFF *and the* CARRIER

  Now, master Sheriff, what is your will with me?
SHERIFF First, pardon me, my lord. A hue and cry
  Hath followed certain men unto this house.
PRINCE What men?
SHERIFF One of them is well known, my gracious lord,   425
  A gross fat man.
CARRIER As fat as butter.

Hal lies to the Sheriff about Falstaff and assures him that Falstaff will be held accountable. Peto finds a tavern bill in the sleeping Falstaff's pocket, mainly for wine. Hal looks to the future wars.

1 The Sheriff (in small groups)

This is the Sheriff's only appearance in the play. Some actors try to turn him into a realistic character (with feelings and a past life). Others argue that the audience should not be interested in him as a person, only for the function he performs in the play: to advance the plot a little and to reveal more of Hal's character.

Remind yourselves of the eight lines he speaks, then talk together about how you think the Sheriff should be played. For example, does he show he disbelieves Hal?

2 The tavern bill

Falstaff has spent only a halfpenny (an 'ob' or 'obolus') on bread, but a great deal on drink. Write a realistic version of Falstaff's tavern bill for use as a stage prop (5s 8d is five shillings and eight pence). In a production, would you change the old-style shillings and pence into modern currency?

3 Acting out Scene 4 (whole class)

Scene 4 is the longest scene in the play, and has four distinct episodes.

lines 1–96: the joke played on Francis

lines 97–269: the joke played on Falstaff

lines 270–399: the Prince and Falstaff play Hal and his father

lines 400–61: Falstaff hides from the Sheriff

Divide the class into four groups. Each group takes responsibility to rehearse and act out one of the episodes.

---

engage my word to thee swear honestly to you
three hundred marks £200
Paul's St Paul's Cathedral
keep close secret, safely
charge of foot company of foot soldiers

death will be ... twelve score he'll die if he has to walk 240 paces
advantage (line 459) interest, extra payment
betimes early

PRINCE The man I do assure you is not here,
       For I myself at this time have employed him.
       And Sheriff, I will engage my word to thee,   430
       That I will by tomorrow dinner-time
       Send him to answer thee, or any man,
       For anything he shall be charged withal.
       And so let me entreat you leave the house.
SHERIFF I will, my lord. There are two gentlemen   435
       Have in this robbery lost three hundred marks.
PRINCE It may be so. If he have robbed these men
       He shall be answerable. And so, farewell.
SHERIFF Good night, my noble lord.
PRINCE I think it is good morrow, is it not?   440
SHERIFF Indeed, my lord, I think it be two o'clock.

                                      Exit [with Carrier]

PRINCE This oily rascal is known as well as Paul's. Go call him forth.
PETO Falstaff! Fast asleep behind the arras, and snorting like a horse.
PRINCE Hark how hard he fetches breath. Search his pockets.

    [Peto] searches his pockets, and finds certain papers

    What hast thou found?   445
PETO Nothing but papers, my lord.
PRINCE Let's see what they be, read them.
[PETO] [*Reads*] *Item a capon*   *2s. 2d.*
    Item sauce   *4d.*
    Item sack two gallons   *5s. 8d.*   450
    Item anchovies and sack after supper *2s. 6d.*
    Item bread   *ob.*
[PRINCE] O monstrous! But one half-pennyworth of bread to this
    intolerable deal of sack? What there is else keep close, we'll read it
    at more advantage. There let him sleep till day. I'll to the court in   455
    the morning. We must all to the wars, and thy place shall be
    honourable. I'll procure this fat rogue a charge of foot, and I know
    his death will be a march of twelve score. The money shall be paid
    back again with advantage. Be with me betimes in the morning, and
    so, good morrow, Peto.   460
PETO Good morrow, good my lord.

                                        Exeunt

Looking back at Act 2
Activities for groups or individuals

1 Sub-plot and main plot

One way of understanding the play is to see the comic sub-plot providing a series of ironic comments on the main plot. Suggest the ways in which each of the following features of the comic sub-plot in Act 2 ironically mirrors or echoes the main political plot of King Henry and the rebels:

- The Carriers' mistrust and suspicion of Gadshill
- The decayed state of the Rochester inn
- Gadshill's confidence that the robbers will escape punishment
- The robbery of the Travellers at Gad's Hill
- The robbery of Falstaff by Hal and Poins
- Falstaff's lies about the robbery, and his play-acting as King Henry.

2 Francis' point of view

Step into role as Francis and tell your story of Prince Hal.

3 Husband and wife: parallel scenes

In *Julius Caesar*, Shakespeare wrote of another wife, Portia, who asks her husband, Brutus, why he is so preoccupied and why he neglects her. Brutus, like Hotspur, is planning the overthrow of a political ruler. Find a copy of *Julius Caesar* and read Act 2 Scene 1, lines 233–309. Then read Kate's lines 31–58 in Scene 3.

Rehearse and present both episodes, inviting your audience to consider the similarities and differences.

4 Tavern signs

Two taverns feature in Act 2, at Rochester and Eastcheap. Design the inn signs that hang outside each tavern.

5 'I'll play Percy'

In Scene 4, lines 94–5, Hal says that he will improvise a play with himself as Hotspur and Falstaff as Hotspur's wife. The play never takes place. Glance back at Scene 3 to remind yourself of how Hotspur talks with his wife (and at Hal's parody in Scene 4, lines 89–94). Then step into role as Hal and Falstaff and improvise their play.

Falstaff plays King Henry as Hal kneels before him.
Find a line from Scene 4 as a caption for this picture.

Mortimer expresses confidence in the rebellion. Hotspur and Glendower praise each other for striking fear into King Henry. Glendower boasts of his earth-shaking birth. Hotspur begins to mock him.

1 Rebels fall out (in groups of four)

In Scene 1, the rebels meet to agree how they will divide up England after they have defeated King Henry. Mortimer will be placed on the throne, and Glendower and the Percy family will each get large areas of the country as the price for supporting him. But Hotspur and Glendower quickly fall to quarrelling.

The first part of the scene shows the personal and political conflict between Hotspur and Glendower. The remainder of the scene is more domestic, showing the relationships of Mortimer and Hotspur with their wives.

Take parts and enact the political section of the scene (lines 1–185). Think about the following:

• How do the rebels enter? Are they wary of each other or determined to show unity from the start?

• Hotspur has forgotten to bring the map (line 5). Let each of the other characters speak their private, unspoken, thoughts about his forgetfulness.

• This is the only time that Mortimer and Glendower appear in the play. After your first reading of all of their lines, decide the type of actor you would cast for each, and how they would be dressed.

• Suggest two or three reasons why Hotspur begins to mock Glendower from line 15. Remember that King Henry described Glendower as 'that great magician', and remind yourself of what Falstaff said about him in Act 2 Scene 4, lines 278–80.

---

the parties sure our allies are reliable
induction beginning (of the rebellion)
Lancaster King Henry (Glendower refuses to call him 'king')

nativity birth
front of heaven sky
cressets torches, beacons in open ironwork baskets

ACT 3 SCENE 1
Wales: Glendower's castle

Enter HOTSPUR, WORCESTER, LORD MORTIMER, OWEN GLENDOWER

MORTIMER These promises are fair, the parties sure,
      And our induction full of prosperous hope.
HOTSPUR Lord Mortimer, and cousin Glendower, will you sit down?
      And uncle Worcester. A plague upon it!
      I have forgot the map.
GLENDOWER   No, here it is.   5
      Sit, cousin Percy, sit, good cousin Hotspur;
      For by that name as oft as Lancaster doth speak of you
      His cheek looks pale, and with a rising sigh
      He wisheth you in heaven.
HOTSPUR   And you in hell,
      As oft as he hears Owen Glendower spoke of.   10
GLENDOWER I cannot blame him. At my nativity
      The front of heaven was full of fiery shapes,
      Of burning cressets, and at my birth
      The frame and huge foundation of the earth
      Shaked like a coward.
HOTSPUR   Why, so it would have done   15
      At the same season if your mother's cat
      Had but kittened, though yourself had never been born.
GLENDOWER I say the earth did shake when I was born.
HOTSPUR And I say the earth was not of my mind,
      If you suppose as fearing you, it shook.   20
GLENDOWER The heavens were all on fire, the earth did tremble –
HOTSPUR O, then the earth shook to see the heavens on fire,
      And not in fear of your nativity.

> *Hotspur explains away earthquakes, but Glendower insists that*
> *miraculous events occurred when he was born, and that he is unlike all*
> *other men. He claims magical powers. Hotspur ridicules his claims.*

1 Glendower the mystic (in pairs)

Hotspur gives a matter-of-fact explanation of the earthquake at the time of Glendower's birth, saying it is like a 'colic' (stomach pain). But Glendower continues to claim that all kinds of strange things happened, which demonstrate he is not an ordinary man.

a Speak Glendower's lines 32–46 in a way to give full expression to all his mystical claims. For example, he might stretch out the word 'extraordinary' (line 38) into six long syllables, and make all kinds of dramatic pauses. Try to give full weight to the following:

line 45 'tedious ways of art' – hard work of magic

line 46 'deep experiments' – magical investigations

b Decide whether you think Glendower speaks only to Hotspur, or to all the characters on stage, or to the audience, or perhaps only to himself, lost in his fantastic imaginings.

c Would you want to make Glendower an obvious figure of fun, making the audience laugh when he says 'the goats ran from the mountains'?

2 Amused contempt, or ...?

Hotspur's replies are intended to puncture Glendower's mystifying bombast. To an aristocratic Englishman like Hotspur, Welsh was considered a barbaric language, like double-Dutch. Find an appropriate tone in which to speak each of Hotspur's replies.

---

teeming fruitful, pregnant
for enlargement striving
  struggling to break free
old beldam grandmother
distemperature disorder
crossings contradictions
roll list

clipped in surrounded by
chides chafes, wears away
read to taught
trace follow
hold me pace match me
the vasty deep Hell

Diseasèd nature oftentimes breaks forth
In strange eruptions, oft the teeming earth   25
Is with a kind of colic pinched and vexed
By the imprisoning of unruly wind
Within her womb, which for enlargement striving
Shakes the old beldam earth, and topples down
Steeples and moss-grown towers. At your birth   30
Our grandam earth, having this distemperature,
In passion shook.
GLENDOWER   Cousin, of many men
I do not bear these crossings. Give me leave
To tell you once again that at my birth
The front of heaven was full of fiery shapes,   35
The goats ran from the mountains, and the herds
Were strangely clamorous to the frighted fields.
These signs have marked me extraordinary,
And all the courses of my life do show
I am not in the roll of common men.   40
Where is he living, clipped in with the sea
That chides the banks of England, Scotland, Wales,
Which calls me pupil or hath read to me?
And bring him out that is but woman's son
Can trace me in the tedious ways of art,   45
And hold me pace in deep experiments.
HOTSPUR I think there's no man speaks better Welsh.
I'll to dinner.
MORTIMER Peace, cousin Percy, you will make him mad.
GLENDOWER I can call spirits from the vasty deep.   50
HOTSPUR Why, so can I, or so can any man,
But will they come when you do call for them?
GLENDOWER Why, I can teach you, cousin, to command the devil.
HOTSPUR And I can teach thee, coz, to shame the devil
By telling truth. Tell truth, and shame the devil.   55
If thou have power to raise him, bring him hither,
And I'll be sworn I have power to shame him hence.
O, while you live, tell truth, and shame the devil!
MORTIMER Come, come, no more of this unprofitable chat.

Glendower boasts of his victories over King Henry and is again mocked by Hotspur. Mortimer explains how the country will be divided between the three rebels. Hotspur has doubts about his share.

1 The division of the kingdom (in small groups)

Shakespeare's audiences were probably horrified at the prospect of dividing up the kingdom. They looked back on the rebellions of Henry IV's reign and the following Wars of the Roses, as a terrible warning of the horrors of civil war. Most probably believed that the unity of the realm was absolutely necessary to order and good government.

a The price of Hotspur's and Glendower's support of Mortimer's claim to the throne is that each shall receive one third of the kingdom. Use lines 66–75 and the map on page 2 to make your own copy of the division (which was originally made by the Archdeacon of Bangor: line 68). Illustrate your map in any way that you think is appropriate.

b Lines 76–7 show that each of the three power-seekers will receive a copy of the contract ('indentures tripartite') that divides the spoils of war between them. Each man will seal the contract ('sealèd interchangeably'). A seal, often set into a ring, contained an image that signified something important about its owner. It was rather like the logo of a modern company. Design one or more of the seals.

c The chaos that results from civil war was explored by Shakespeare not only in his history plays but also in *King Lear*. That play begins with Lear producing a map which divides his kingdom into three. Disaster follows Lear's division of his kingdom. Find a copy of *King Lear* and compare Act 1 Scene 1, lines 32–122 with the lines opposite.

Henry Bullingbrook King Henry (Glendower again refuses to say 'king')
made head gathered an army
Bootless defeated, without booty
agues fevers

in my conduct under my protection
a world of water shed many tears
moiety portion, share
monstrous scantle huge slice

GLENDOWER Three times hath Henry Bullingbrook made head   60
　　　　　Against my power, thrice from the banks of Wye
　　　　　And sandy-bottomed Severn have I sent him
　　　　　Bootless home, and weather-beaten back.
HOTSPUR Home without boots, and in foul weather too!
　　　　　How scapes he agues, in the devil's name?   65
GLENDOWER Come, here is the map, shall we divide our right
　　　　　According to our threefold order taken?
MORTIMER The Archdeacon hath divided it
　　　　　Into three limits very equally.
　　　　　England, from Trent and Severn hitherto,   70
　　　　　By south and east is to my part assigned.
　　　　　All westward, Wales beyond the Severn shore,
　　　　　And all the fertile land within that bound,
　　　　　To Owen Glendower. And, dear coz, to you
　　　　　The remnant northward lying off from Trent.   75
　　　　　And our indentures tripartite are drawn,
　　　　　Which being sealèd interchangeably –
　　　　　A business that this night may execute –
　　　　　Tomorrow, cousin Percy, you and I
　　　　　And my good Lord of Worcester will set forth   80
　　　　　To meet your father and the Scottish power,
　　　　　As is appointed us, at Shrewsbury.
　　　　　My father Glendower is not ready yet,
　　　　　Nor shall we need his help these fourteen days.
　　　　　[*To Glendower*] Within that space you may have drawn together
　　　　　Your tenants, friends, and neighbouring gentlemen.
GLENDOWER A shorter time shall send me to you, lords,
　　　　　And in my conduct shall your ladies come,
　　　　　From whom you now must steal and take no leave,
　　　　　For there will be a world of water shed   90
　　　　　Upon the parting of your wives and you.
HOTSPUR Methinks my moiety, north from Burton here,
　　　　　In quantity equals not one of yours.
　　　　　See how this river comes me cranking in,
　　　　　And cuts me from the best of all my land   95
　　　　　A huge half-moon, a monstrous scantle out.

Hotspur wants to divert the River Trent to give him a better share of the land. Glendower protests. Hotspur scorns the music and poetry that Glendower values. Glendower agrees to have the river's course changed.

1 To pause or not to pause (in pairs)

There is a theatrical convention that when a line is shared by two speakers, there is no pause between the two voices. Another convention is that when Shakespeare writes a half line, there is a pause before the next character speaks (equivalent to the 'missing' words).

Experiment with different ways of speaking lines 111–15 to discover whether you think pauses are or are not appropriate in this confrontation between Hotspur and Glendower.

2 More mockery

True to form, Hotspur mocks music and poetry in lines 123–9. He claims to prefer the crying of cats, scraping of metal ('a brazen canstick turned' is the noise of a brass candlestick being made), or the screeching of unlubricated wheels ('grate on the axle-tree'). Give one or two reasons for your decision about whether or not you think Hotspur really means what he says.

3 More aspects of Glendower

The mystical Glendower reveals another side of his character: the musical skill he acquired at the English court, where he set songs to music ('framèd to the harp'). He uses that ability to criticise Hotspur ('A virtue that was never seen in you').

But although he seems fiercely opposed to Hotspur, he suddenly agrees (line 130) to Hotspur's demand to have the course of the River Trent altered. Give your own view on why you think he gives in to Hotspur.

---

so rich a bottom such a fertile valley
like advantage the same result
Gelding ... continent cutting off the opposite bank
charge cost, gunpowder

trench him dig a new river channel
metre ballad-mongers sellers of popular songs
forced gait awkward walking

        I'll have the current in this place dammed up,
        And here the smug and silver Trent shall run
        In a new channel fair and evenly.
        It shall not wind with such a deep indent,   100
        To rob me of so rich a bottom here.
GLENDOWER Not wind? It shall, it must – you see it doth.
MORTIMER Yea,
        But mark how he bears his course, and runs me up
        With like advantage on the other side,   105
        Gelding the opposèd continent as much
        As on the other side it takes from you.
WORCESTER Yea, but a little charge will trench him here,
        And on this north side win this cape of land,
        And then he runs straight and even.   110
HOTSPUR I'll have it so, a little charge will do it.
GLENDOWER I'll not have it altered.
HOTSPUR   Will not you?
GLENDOWER No, nor you shall not.
HOTSPUR   Who shall say me nay?
GLENDOWER Why, that will I.
HOTSPUR Let me not understand you then, speak it in Welsh.   115
GLENDOWER I can speak English, lord, as well as you,
        For I was trained up in the English court,
        Where, being but young, I framèd to the harp
        Many an English ditty lovely well,
        And gave the tongue a helpful ornament –   120
        A virtue that was never seen in you.
HOTSPUR Marry and I am glad of it with all my heart!
        I had rather be a kitten and cry 'mew'
        Than one of these same metre ballad-mongers.
        I had rather hear a brazen canstick turned,   125
        Or a dry wheel grate on the axle-tree,
        And that would set my teeth nothing on edge,
        Nothing so much as mincing poetry.
        'Tis like the forced gait of a shuffling nag.
GLENDOWER Come, you shall have Trent turned.   130

Hotspur gives up his claim to more land. He tells how Glendower's mysticism angers and bores him. Mortimer defends Glendower, praising his many qualities.

1 'I do not care'

Hotspur abruptly abandons his claim to more land. But why? Imagine that the actor playing Hotspur says to you, 'I don't understand this. Surely Hotspur should say "honour", not "bargain" at line 133. Why does he say "bargain"? Can I change it in performance?' Make your reply.

2 Two views of Glendower (in pairs)

Two very different views of Glendower are given in lines 141–70. Mortimer praises him, but Hotspur is bored by Glendower's stories. He says that rather than listen to Glendower, he would prefer to eat the cheapest of foods ('cheese and garlic') and live in a noisy windmill.

Take parts as Hotspur and Mortimer and speak the lines in a way that expresses their characters as much as Glendower's.

3 Merlin's prophecies

Merlin was the legendary wizard to King Arthur (lines 142–7). Perhaps Glendower was talking about the prophecy that King Henry ('the moldwarp' or mole) would be defeated by Glendower, Hotspur and Mortimer, whose shields respectively bore the emblems of the dragon, the lion and the wolf.

Step into role as Glendower and invent a mythical prophecy that involves all the creatures Hotspur mentions (for example, a griffin is a mythical beast with the head of an eagle and the body of a lion). Don't worry about how fantastic your prophecy is, after all, Hotspur dismisses it as 'skimble-skamble stuff'. But you might wish to try to relate it to the political plot of the play.

---

cavil argue, wrangle
Break with Tell, inform
moulten featherless (moulted)
couching sitting with head raised
ramping rearing up on hind legs
lackeys servants

railing nagging
cates cakes, dainties
strange concealments magic secrets
scope instinct, temperament
come 'cross contradict, mock

HOTSPUR I do not care, I'll give thrice so much land
       To any well-deserving friend.
       But in the way of bargain, mark ye me,
       I'll cavil on the ninth part of a hair.
       Are the indentures drawn? Shall we be gone?   135
GLENDOWER The moon shines fair, you may away by night.
       I'll haste the writer, and withal
       Break with your wives of your departure hence.
       I am afraid my daughter will run mad,
       So much she doteth on her Mortimer.   *Exit* 140
MORTIMER Fie, cousin Percy, how you cross my father!
HOTSPUR I cannot choose. Sometime he angers me
       With telling me of the moldwarp and the ant,
       Of the dreamer Merlin and his prophecies,
       And of a dragon and a finless fish,   145
       A clip-winged griffin and a moulten raven,
       A couching lion and a ramping cat,
       And such a deal of skimble-skamble stuff
       As puts me from my faith. I tell you what –
       He held me last night at least nine hours   150
       In reckoning up the several devils' names
       That were his lackeys. I cried 'Hum', and 'Well, go to!'
       But marked him not a word. O, he is as tedious
       As a tired horse, a railing wife,
       Worse than a smoky house. I had rather live   155
       With cheese and garlic in a windmill, far,
       Than feed on cates and have him talk to me
       In any summer house in Christendom.
MORTIMER In faith, he is a worthy gentleman,
       Exceedingly well read, and profited   160
       In strange concealments, valiant as a lion,
       And wondrous affable, and as bountiful
       As mines of India. Shall I tell you, cousin?
       He holds your temper in a high respect
       And curbs himself even of his natural scope   165
       When you come 'cross his humour, faith he does.
       I warrant you that man is not alive
       Might so have tempted him as you have done
       Without the taste of danger and reproof.
       But do not use it oft, let me entreat you.   170

Worcester urges Hotspur to restrain his outspokenness because it detracts from his nobility. Mortimer praises his wife's Welsh language and regrets his inability to speak Welsh in reply.

1 Suffering fools gladly (in pairs)

Hotspur's treatment of Glendower is an example of someone who says he 'cannot suffer fools gladly'. Worcester identifies what such behaviour often shows such a person to be: very self-opinionated and thoroughly objectionable.

a Practise speaking Worcester's lines to bring out his criticisms in lines 177–9 ('harsh rage' to 'disdain'). Consider each criticism in turn and say whether you think it truly describes Hotspur (for example, 'want of government' means lack of self-control).

b Have a conversation together on whether you think 'not suffering fools gladly' is a good or bad aspect of someone's character.

c Hotspur replies 'Well, I am schooled' ('Yes, I'll learn the lesson') to Worcester's advice. But do you think he means it? Speak line 184 in different ways (sincerely, sarcastically and so on).

2 Act it out (in groups of five)

A change in mood occurs with the entry of the wives of Hotspur and Mortimer. Take parts as Mortimer, Glendower, Hotspur, Lady Mortimer and Kate (Lady Percy). Read through from line 185 to the end of the scene.

Whoever plays Mortimer's wife and Glendower may have to improvise their Welsh. What would you do if you were putting on a production and no one in the cast could speak Welsh?

---

wilful-blame headstrong and blameworthy
haunting characterising
Beguiling ... commendation robbing them of reputation
in your conduct under your protection

harlotry untrustworthy woman (spoken affectionately?)
parley military conference
feeling disputation conversation of love
ravishing division delightful musical variations

WORCESTER In faith, my lord, you are too wilful-blame,
        And since your coming hither have done enough
        To put him quite besides his patience.
        You must needs learn, lord, to amend this fault.
        Though sometimes it show greatness, courage, blood –   175
        And that's the dearest grace it renders you –
        Yet oftentimes it doth present harsh rage,
        Defect of manners, want of government,
        Pride, haughtiness, opinion, and disdain,
        The least of which haunting a nobleman   180
        Loseth men's hearts and leaves behind a stain
        Upon the beauty of all parts besides,
        Beguiling them of commendation.
HOTSPUR Well, I am schooled – good manners be your speed!
        Here come our wives, and let us take our leave.   185

      Enter GLENDOWER *with the* LADIES

MORTIMER This is the deadly spite that angers me,
        My wife can speak no English, I no Welsh.
GLENDOWER My daughter weeps, she'll not part with you,
        She'll be a soldier too, she'll to the wars.
MORTIMER Good father, tell her that she and my aunt Percy   190
        Shall follow in your conduct speedily.
  Glendower speaks to her in Welsh, and she answers him in the same
GLENDOWER She is desperate here, a peevish, self-willed harlotry,
        one that no persuasion can do good upon.
        The lady speaks in Welsh
MORTIMER I understand thy looks, that pretty Welsh
        Which thou pourest down from these swelling heavens   195
        I am too perfect in, and but for shame
        In such a parley should I answer thee.
        The lady [speaks] again in Welsh
        I understand thy kisses, and thou mine,
        And that's a feeling disputation,
        But I will never be a truant, love,   200
        Till I have learnt thy language, for thy tongue
        Makes Welsh as sweet as ditties highly penned,
        Sung by a fair queen in a summer's bower
        With ravishing division to her lute.

Glendower says that his daughter wants Mortimer to lie down and listen to her sing. He calls for music. Hotspur refuses to be serious or tender.

Glendower, with his daughter and Mortimer. Speak lines 207–15, then think about how far you agree with the view that they show Glendower to be a true poet.

1 Music and magic

In Shakespeare's theatre, the musicians might have played in the gallery at the back of the stage. Today, most productions try to make the music interlude as magical as possible. How would you stage it?

---

melt weep, behave lovingly
wanton rushes abundant reeds
(which were used as a floor
covering)
heavenly-harnessed team
sun (in mythology, drawn by a
team of horses)

book contract
drawn written in full
thousand leagues 3000 miles
(5000 kilometres)
humours moods
brach hunting dog

GLENDOWER Nay, if you melt, then will she run mad.   205
                    The lady speaks again in Welsh
MORTIMER O, I am ignorance itself in this!
GLENDOWER She bids you on the wanton rushes lay you down,
                    And rest your gentle head upon her lap,
                    And she will sing the song that pleaseth you,
                    And on your eyelids crown the god of sleep,   210
                    Charming your blood with pleasing heaviness,
                    Making such difference 'twixt wake and sleep
                    As is the difference betwixt day and night,
                    The hour before the heavenly-harnessed team
                    Begins his golden progress in the east.   215
MORTIMER With all my heart I'll sit and hear her sing,
                    By that time will our book, I think, be drawn.
GLENDOWER Do so, and those musicians that shall play to you
                    Hang in the air a thousand leagues from hence,
                    And straight they shall be here. Sit, and attend.   220
HOTSPUR Come, Kate, thou art perfect in lying down.
                    Come, quick, quick, that I may lay my head in thy lap.
LADY PERCY Go, ye giddy goose.
                    The music plays
HOTSPUR Now I perceive the devil understands Welsh,
                    And 'tis no marvel he is so humorous,   225
                    By'r lady, he is a good musician.
LADY PERCY Then should you be nothing but musical,
                    For you are altogether governed by humours.
                    Lie still, ye thief, and hear the lady sing in Welsh.
HOTSPUR I had rather hear Lady my brach howl in Irish.   230
LADY PERCY Wouldst thou have thy head broken?
HOTSPUR No.
LADY PERCY Then be still.
HOTSPUR Neither, 'tis a woman's fault.
LADY PERCY Now, God help thee!   235
HOTSPUR To the Welsh lady's bed.
LADY PERCY What's that?
HOTSPUR Peace, she sings.

Kate refuses to sing. Hotspur criticises her for using a mild oath that he thinks is suitable only to middle-class women. He determines to leave shortly after the contract is signed.

1 A soldier and a snob?

Hotspur criticises Kate for using a mild oath which he says is only suitable for 'a comfit-maker's wife' (the wife of a maker of sweets and candy). He mimics other sayings of such women and asks Kate to swear more strongly. She should leave mild oaths to those respectable London citizens who, in their Sunday best trimmed with velvet, strolled in the parish of Finsbury.

What is your response to Hotspur's mockery of persons of a lower social class than his own?

2 Man and wife (in pairs)

Take parts as Hotspur and his wife and speak lines 221–54. Afterwards, look at the picture on page 125 then talk together about the following:

a Are they equal partners?

b Do they really love each other?

c Why does he mock music and tease his wife?

d Why does Kate refuse to sing?

e Is Hotspur glad or sorry at his wife's refusal to sing?

f How does Hotspur leave the stage? Does he kiss his wife?

g How does Kate respond to Hotspur's departure? How does she finally leave at the end of the scene?

After your responses to the above questions, write a single paragraph to describe their relationship.

---

in good sooth in truth
sarcenet surety weak guarantees (sarcenet is fine silk)
Finsbury a respectable area of London

pepper-gingerbread cheap biscuits
tailor (tailors were traditionally good singers)
be redbreast teacher teach a robin to sing

Here the lady sings a Welsh song
Come, Kate, I'll have your song too.
LADY PERCY Not mine, in good sooth.   240
HOTSPUR Not yours, in good sooth! Heart, you swear like a comfit-
maker's wife – 'Not you, in good sooth!' and 'As true as I live!' and
'As God shall mend me!', and 'As sure as day!' –
    And givest such sarcenet surety for thy oaths
    As if thou never walk'st further than Finsbury.   245
    Swear me, Kate, like a lady as thou art,
    A good mouth-filling oath, and leave 'In sooth',
    And such protest of pepper-gingerbread,
    To velvet-guards, and Sunday citizens.
    Come, sing.   250
LADY PERCY I will not sing.
HOTSPUR 'Tis the next way to turn tailor, or be redbreast teacher.
    An the indentures be drawn I'll away within these two
    hours. And so, come in when ye will.
    Exit
GLENDOWER Come, come, Lord Mortimer, you are as slow   255
    As hot Lord Percy is on fire to go.
    By this our book is drawn – we'll but seal,
    And then to horse immediately.
MORTIMER With all my heart.
                          Exeunt

King Henry wonders whether God is punishing him through the bad behaviour of his son. He asks how Hal can keep such low company. Hal hopes that truth will outweigh scandalous tittle-tattle.

1 First read through (in pairs or small groups)

To gain a first impression of the whole scene, take parts and read it through without pausing. Because some speeches are long, you may find it helpful to share King Henry's lines between several speakers, each reading only a short section in turn. Two points to consider:

a Henry wonders whether Hal's misbehaviour is a punishment for his own sins ('displeasing service' and 'mistreadings' could refer to his own misdeeds in deposing King Richard and seizing the throne). Suggest how Henry speaks lines 12–17 with his many repetitions of 'such', and the long list of negative qualities ('inordinate and low desires', 'poor', 'bare', and so on).

b Henry is both king and father, just as Hal is both Prince and son. Think about how these personal and public roles might affect their behaviour. Does Henry (as king) sit on the throne and keep Hal at a distance, or does he (as father) sit close to him and use an affectionate, regretful tone. Does Hal kneel before his father the king? Does he try to make some kind of physical contact?

2 Reporting rumours

Hal admits to some offences ('faulty wandered and irregular') but hopes that when all the truth is known he can disprove the many false stories told by 'smiling pickthanks, and base newsmongers' (flattering tell-tales and gossips). Today, such rumours would probably be spread through newspapers. Invent a few headlines to introduce news items about the scandalous behaviour of the Prince of Wales.

---

give us leave leave the room
presently shortly
secret doom fateful judgement
blood children
scourge harsh punishment
passages of life life style

inordinate excessive, unworthy
rude society disreputable friends
grafted joined
hold their level rank equally
extenuation mitigation, pardon

ACT 3 SCENE 2
London: King Henry's palace

Enter the KING, PRINCE OF WALES, *and others*

KING Lords, give us leave. The Prince of Wales and I
        Must have some private conference – but be near at hand,
        For we shall presently have need of you.
                                       Exeunt Lords
        I know not whether God will have it so
        For some displeasing service I have done,   5
        That in his secret doom out of my blood
        He'll breed revengement and a scourge for me.
        But thou dost in thy passages of life
        Make me believe that thou art only marked
        For the hot vengeance and the rod of heaven,   10
        To punish my mistreadings. Tell me else,
        Could such inordinate and low desires,
        Such poor, such bare, such lewd, such mean attempts,
        Such barren pleasures, rude society,
        As thou art matched withal, and grafted to,   15
        Accompany the greatness of thy blood
        And hold their level with thy princely heart?
PRINCE So please your majesty, I would I could
        Quit all offences with as clear excuse
        As well as I am doubtless I can purge   20
        Myself of many I am charged withal.
        Yet such extenuation let me beg
        As, in reproof of many tales devised,
        Which oft the ear of greatness needs must hear,
        By smiling pickthanks, and base newsmongers,   25
        I may for some things true, wherein my youth
        Hath faulty wandered and irregular,
        Find pardon on my true submission.

King Henry tells that Hal's misdeeds have resulted in his son's loss of authority. Henry describes how he rarely appeared in public, unlike King Richard, who was over-familiar with impudent, joking fools.

1 Hal's misdeeds

King Henry's speech has four distinct sections beginning at lines 29, 39, 60 and 85. They deal respectively with Hal's lost reputation, King Henry's behaviour, King Richard II's behaviour, and a rebuke to Hal.

Henry first uses an image from falconry ('wing', 'flight') to imply that Hal does not measure up to his ancestors. Hal's misbehaviour has resulted in him losing his place on the king's Council, losing the trust and loyalty of the court, and being thought a no-hoper, whose downfall everyone can foresee ('forethink thy fall').

In what tone of voice might Henry speak lines 29–38: sadly, angrily, accusingly ...?

2 A lesson in statecraft (in small groups)

From line 39 King Henry embarks on a lesson on how kings should behave: avoid mixing freely with the people, be seldom seen, make your rare appearances magnificent occasions ('Seldom, but sumptuous'). If he had been 'common-hackneyed' (vulgarly familiar) with the people, says Henry, they would have remained loyal 'to possession' (King Richard II), and left him 'in reputeless (dishonourable) banishment'. It was his very rare appearances that made him wondered at.

Experiment with different ways of speaking Henry's lines 39–59: as a king to his heir, as a television broadcast, as a businessman advising a newly appointed manager, and so on.

After your practical explorations, talk together about what you think of Henry's advice for leaders.

Opinion public opinion
pluck allegiance from inspire
  loyalty in
salutations greetings
a robe pontifical the Pope's robe
skipping frivolous
rash bavin wits foolish friends
  ('bavin' is firewood)

carded his state debased his
  dignity (to 'card' is to dilute a
  drink)
stand the push tolerate the
  insolence
beardless vain comparative
  young boastful joker

KING God pardon thee! Yet let me wonder, Harry,
　　　　At thy affections, which do hold a wing　　　　　　　　30
　　　　Quite from the flight of all thy ancestors.
　　　　Thy place in Council thou hast rudely lost,
　　　　Which by thy younger brother is supplied,
　　　　And art almost an alien to the hearts
　　　　Of all the court and princes of my blood.　　　　　　35
　　　　The hope and expectation of thy time
　　　　Is ruined, and the soul of every man
　　　　Prophetically do forethink thy fall.
　　　　Had I so lavish of my presence been,
　　　　So common-hackneyed in the eyes of men,　　　　　40
　　　　So stale and cheap to vulgar company,
　　　　Opinion, that did help me to the crown,
　　　　Had still kept loyal to possession,
　　　　And left me in reputeless banishment,
　　　　A fellow of no mark nor likelihood.　　　　　　　　45
　　　　By being seldom seen, I could not stir
　　　　But like a comet I was wondered at,
　　　　That men would tell their children, 'This is he!'
　　　　Others would say, 'Where, which is Bullingbrook?'
　　　　And then I stole all courtesy from heaven,　　　　　50
　　　　And dressed myself in such humility
　　　　That I did pluck allegiance from men's hearts,
　　　　Loud shouts and salutations from their mouths,
　　　　Even in the presence of the crownèd King.
　　　　Thus did I keep my person fresh and new,　　　　　55
　　　　My presence, like a robe pontifical,
　　　　Ne'er seen but wondered at, and so my state,
　　　　Seldom, but sumptuous, showed like a feast,
　　　　And won by rareness such solemnity.
　　　　The skipping King, he ambled up and down,　　　　60
　　　　With shallow jesters, and rash bavin wits,
　　　　Soon kindled and soon burnt, carded his state,
　　　　Mingled his royalty with capering fools,
　　　　Had his great name profanèd with their scorns,
　　　　And gave his countenance against his name　　　　　65
　　　　To laugh at gibing boys, and stand the push
　　　　Of every beardless vain comparative,

Henry continues to condemn King Richard for being too over-familiar and too often seen. He accuses Hal of the same fault and says that Hotspur better deserves to become king.

1 Don't do it!

Give your reaction to what one student wrote: 'Henry's condemnation of King Richard (lines 60–84) is filled with images and words that lower Richard's status. What it all adds up to in modern times is: never appear on chat shows on TV. They will just make fun of you!'

2 Imagery (in pairs)

Henry uses a wide range of images in lines 29–84. Here are some in the order in which they appear in the script: falconry, a comet, heaven, churchmen's costume, a feast, firewood, diluting drink, honey, cuckoo, the sun, overeating. Remind yourself of each image, then choose two that particularly appeal to you and say why they work well.

3 Father and son

King Henry's feelings as a father show through in lines 87–91, as tears express his 'foolish tenderness'. Henry says that Hotspur better deserves the crown of England because of his personal merits. Although he has no legitimate right to the throne ('no right, nor colour like to right') he can raise a mighty army and command experienced noblemen.

Henry again hints at his own dubious right to the throne when he describes Hal as 'the shadow of succession'. One interpretation is 'dubious heir to the throne'. Try to give one or two different interpretations of this expression in line 99.

Enfeoffed surrendered
surfeited became over-full and sick
community over-familiarity
in his face in the king's presence
cloudy sullen

vile participation keeping lowly company
to boot also
hath more worthy interest to the state better deserves the crown
harness men in armour

Grew a companion to the common streets,
Enfeoffed himself to popularity,
That, being daily swallowed by men's eyes, 70
They surfeited with honey, and began
To loathe the taste of sweetness, whereof a little
More than a little is by much too much.
So, when he had occasion to be seen,
He was but as the cuckoo is in June, 75
Heard, not regarded; seen, but with such eyes
As, sick and blunted with community,
Afford no extraordinary gaze,
Such as is bent on sun-like majesty
When it shines seldom in admiring eyes, 80
But rather drowsed and hung their eyelids down,
Slept in his face, and rendered such aspect
As cloudy men use to their adversaries,
Being with his presence glutted, gorged, and full.
And in that very line, Harry, standest thou, 85
For thou hast lost thy princely privilege
With vile participation. Not an eye
But is a-weary of thy common sight,
Save mine, which hath desired to see thee more,
Which now doth that I would not have it do, 90
Make blind itself with foolish tenderness.

PRINCE I shall hereafter, my thrice-gracious lord,
Be more myself.

KING   For all the world
As thou art to this hour was Richard then
When I from France set foot at Ravenspurgh, 95
And even as I was then is Percy now.
Now by my sceptre, and my soul to boot,
He hath more worthy interest to the state
Than thou the shadow of succession.
For of no right, nor colour like to right, 100
He doth fill fields with harness in the realm,
Turns head against the lion's armèd jaws,
And being no more in debt to years than thou
Leads ancient lords and reverend bishops on
To bloody battles, and to bruising arms. 105

King Henry continues to praise Hotspur for his defeat of the great soldier
Douglas. He fears Hal might even join Hotspur in rebellion. Hal swears
to defeat Hotspur and acquire his honour.

1 A final insult to Hal

Henry describes Douglas as the finest soldier in the Christian world.
He pictures Hotspur as an infant Mars, a young god of war wrapped
like a new-born baby ('in swaddling clothes'). Douglas has now joined
the other rebels, adding to the clamour against the king ('fill the mouth
of deep defiance up'). After listing the rebels, Henry adds a final
condemnation against Hal: he too may join the rebels and fight for pay.

Suggest why the images of 'dog his heels, and curtsy at his frowns'
(line 127) would be deeply insulting to Hal.

2 Hal's reply

Hal finally replies to his father's criticism. His intention is to assure his
father that he will regain his good reputation and kill Hotspur. Practise
ways of speaking Hal's lines 129–59 using the following to help you:

- How long might Hal pause before beginning his reply?
- Is his style of speaking quiet and assured, or passionate and threatening, or ...?
- Hal swears to redeem his honour by killing Hotspur. Lines 135–7 contain a chilling image of redemption as Hal pictures himself washing away his sins in Hotspur's blood. He goes on to wish his own shames were double and Hotspur had even more honour, so that his victory and redemption will become more glorious. What movements and gestures might he use to accompany his vows?

hot incursions lightning raids	**Base inclination** dishonourable
chief majority ... capital highest	tendencies
military honours	**start of spleen** angry impulses
Discomfited defeated	**swayed** influenced
Enlargèd released	**favours** helmet ribbons
Capitulate sign agreements	**unthought-of** undervalued
vassal slavish	**helm** helmet

What never-dying honour hath he got
Against renownèd Douglas! Whose high deeds,
Whose hot incursions and great name in arms,
Holds from all soldiers chief majority
And military title capital   110
Through all the kingdoms that acknowledge Christ.
Thrice hath this Hotspur, Mars in swaddling clothes,
This infant warrior, in his enterprises
Discomfited great Douglas, taken him once,
Enlargèd him, and made a friend of him,   115
To fill the mouth of deep defiance up,
And shake the peace and safety of our throne.
And what say you to this? Percy, Northumberland,
The Archbishop's Grace of York, Douglas, Mortimer,
Capitulate against us and are up.   120
But wherefore do I tell these news to thee?
Why, Harry, do I tell thee of my foes,
Which art my nearest and dearest enemy?
Thou that art like enough, through vassal fear,
Base inclination, and the start of spleen,   125
To fight against me under Percy's pay,
To dog his heels, and curtsy at his frowns,
To show how much thou art degenerate.
PRINCE Do not think it so, you shall not find it so;
And God forgive them that so much have swayed   130
Your majesty's good thoughts away from me!
I will redeem all this on Percy's head,
And in the closing of some glorious day
Be bold to tell you that I am your son,
When I will wear a garment all of blood,   135
And stain my favours in a bloody mask,
Which, washed away, shall scour my shame with it.
And that shall be the day, whene'er it lights,
That this same child of honour and renown,
This gallant Hotspur, this all-praisèd knight,   140
And your unthought-of Harry chance to meet.
For every honour sitting on his helm,
Would they were multitudes, and on my head
My shames redoubled. For the time will come
That I shall make this northern youth exchange   145
His glorious deeds for my indignities.

Hal vows to take all Hotspur's honours by defeating him in battle.
Henry rejoices, gives him high command, and issues orders to meet the
other army commanders at Bridgnorth.

1 Hal versus Hotspur (in pairs)

a Hal uses a commercial image in lines 147–52. Find all the words
to do with commerce and business and speak them with
contempt. Do you think Hal would speak them in such a way?

b 'This in the name of God ...'. How does Hal swear his oath?
Invent a brief ceremony he might use to accompany line 153.

c Suggest how Henry delivers line 160: his tone, gestures, and so
on.

2 Another Mortimer?

In line 164, Shakespeare portrays Lord Mortimer of Scotland as a
major supporter of the king. But no such character existed historically.
See page 200 for ways in which Shakespeare creates his own version of
history.

3 The voice of command?

King Henry's final speech is full of military information and commands.
Work out line by line how to stage it, perhaps using a copy of the map
on page 2 as a stage prop to help Henry issue his orders.

Would you show Henry as a military leader in full control of the
situation, issuing his orders with brisk authority? Or might he be less
confident, and work out what to do slowly, point by point, with long
pauses for thought?

---

factor agent
engross buy, collect
reckoning account
salve heal
intemperance hot-headed
  behaviour
bands debts, bonds

charge and sovereign trust
  command of an army and my
  confidence
head army
advertisement news
Our business valuèd by my
  calculation
Advantage ... delay there's
  danger in delay

Percy is but my factor, good my lord,
To engross up glorious deeds on my behalf,
And I will call him to so strict account
That he shall render every glory up,   150
Yea, even the slightest worship of his time,
Or I will tear the reckoning from his heart.
This in the name of God I promise here,
The which if He be pleased I shall perform,
I do beseech your majesty may salve   155
The long-grown wounds of my intemperance.
If not, the end of life cancels all bands,
And I will die a hundred thousand deaths
Ere break the smallest parcel of this vow.
KING A hundred thousand rebels die in this.   160
　　　　Thou shalt have charge and sovereign trust herein.

[*Enter* BLUNT]

How now, good Blunt? Thy looks are full of speed.
BLUNT So hath the business that I come to speak of.
　　　　Lord Mortimer of Scotland hath sent word
　　　　That Douglas and the English rebels met   165
　　　　The eleventh of this month at Shrewsbury.
　　　　A mighty and a fearful head they are,
　　　　If promises be kept on every hand,
　　　　As ever offered foul play in a state.
KING The Earl of Westmoreland set forth today,   170
　　　　With him my son, Lord John of Lancaster,
　　　　For this advertisement is five days old.
　　　　On Wednesday next, Harry, you shall set forward.
　　　　On Thursday we ourselves will march.
　　　　Our meeting is Bridgnorth, and, Harry, you   175
　　　　Shall march through Gloucestershire, by which account,
　　　　Our business valuèd, some twelve days hence
　　　　Our general forces at Bridgnorth shall meet.
　　　　Our hands are full of business, let's away,
　　　　Advantage feeds him fat while men delay.   180

Exeunt

Falstaff complains that he is losing weight, and says he will repent. He jokingly recalls his past life-style, then develops elaborate fantasies about Bardolph's face.

1 Pretending to be serious (in pairs)

Lines 1–15 show Falstaff using some of his favourite techniques to get laughs. He adopts the tone of a virtuous man who finds himself surrounded by wickedness. He pretends to criticise himself, and says that he is thin. He puts on a serious face, vowing he will repent, and claiming he has been ruined by villainous companions. But at the same time he is always mocking his own pretended seriousness.

Explore ways of speaking Falstaff's lines 1–15 to bring out the humour. For example, make the most of the opportunities to pause in lines 12, 13 and 14.

2 Bardolph's face (in pairs)

Bardolph has been a heavy drinker for many years, and his face shows it. Falstaff makes all kinds of fantastic comparisons saying it reminds him of:

- the lantern on the stern deck ('poop') of a flagship ('admiral')
- a romantic tale of chivalry ('Knight of the Burning Lamp')
- a skull engraved on a ring as a reminder of death (*'memento mori'*)
- the parable in the Bible of Dives, a rich man dressed in purple, who finally burned in the fires of Hell
- a will of the wisp (*'ignis fatuus'*)
- a firework or explosive charge ('wildfire')
- a torch-lit victory procession ('triumph')
- a legendary lizard that lived in fire ('salamander').

Take parts and speak lines 16–39, then find a practical way of illustrating Falstaff's comparisons (for example, as a series of illustrations).

---

last action (the robbery at Gad's Hill)
bate lose weight
apple-john shrivelled apple
in some liking still fit, inclined

peppercorn tiny grain
Diced gambled
bawdy-house brothel
compass order, limit
given over wicked

Act 3   Scene 3
Eastcheap: the Boar's Head Tavern

Enter FALSTAFF *and* BARDOLPH

FALSTAFF Bardolph, am I not fallen away vilely since this last action?
Do I not bate? Do I not dwindle? Why, my skin hangs about me
like an old lady's loose gown. I am withered like an old apple-john.
Well, I'll repent, and that suddenly, while I am in some liking. I
shall be out of heart shortly, and then I shall have no strength to   5
repent. And I have not forgotten what the inside of a church is
made of, I am a peppercorn, a brewer's horse. The inside of a
church! Company, villainous company, hath been the spoil of me.
BARDOLPH Sir John, you are so fretful you cannot live long.
FALSTAFF Why, there is it. Come, sing me a bawdy song, make me   10
merry. I was as virtuously given as a gentleman need to be. Virtuous
enough. Swore little. Diced not above seven times – a week. Went
to a bawdy-house not above once in a quarter – of an hour. Paid
money that I borrowed – three or four times. Lived well, and in good
compass: and now I live out of all order, out of all compass.   15
BARDOLPH Why, you are so fat, Sir John, that you must needs be out
of all compass, out of all reasonable compass, Sir John.
FALSTAFF Do thou amend thy face, and I'll amend my life. Thou art
our admiral, thou bearest the lantern in the poop, but 'tis in the
nose of thee. Thou art the Knight of the Burning Lamp.   20
BARDOLPH Why, Sir John, my face does you no harm.
FALSTAFF No, I'll be sworn, I make as good use of it as many a man doth
of a death's-head, or a *memento mori.* I never see thy face but I think
upon hell-fire, and Dives that lived in purple: for there he is in his
robes, burning, burning. If thou wert any way given to virtue, I   25
would swear by thy face. My oath should be 'By this fire, that's
God's angel!' But thou art altogether given over, and wert indeed,
but for the light in thy face, the son of utter darkness. When thou
ran'st up Gad's Hill in the night to catch my horse, if I did not think
thou hadst been an *ignis fatuus,* or a ball of wildfire, there's no   30
purchase in money. O, thou art a perpetual triumph, an everlasting

Falstaff continues to mock Bardolph's face. The Hostess denies that any of her staff picked Falstaff's pocket, and reminds him that he owes her money. Falstaff refuses to pay, and exaggerates his losses.

'Go to, you are a woman, go!'
Just how does Falstaff deliver line 47?

1 What is their relationship? (in pairs)

The Hostess reminds Falstaff of his debts, but he won't even give her a straight answer! He calls her 'dame Partlet the hen' (a traditional nickname for a fussy woman), and he says the shirts she gave him were 'Dowlas' (coarse linen), so he gave them away to bakers' wives to make 'bolters' (cloth for sieving flour).

As you speak the exchanges between Falstaff and the Hostess, try to work out how each feels about the other.

mark two thirds of £1	**beguile** cheat
links blazing flares	**holland** fine linen
chandler's candle seller's	**ell** 45 inches (110 cm)
salamander see page 114	**denier** one tenth of one penny
'Sblood By God's blood	**younker** greenhorn, inexperienced
tithe tenth part	youngster

bonfire-light! Thou hast saved me a thousand marks in links and
torches, walking with thee in the night betwixt tavern and tavern.
But the sack that thou hast drunk me would have bought me lights
as good cheap at the dearest chandler's in Europe. I have maintained   35
that salamander of yours with fire any time this two-and-thirty
years, God reward me for it!
BARDOLPH 'Sblood, I would my face were in your belly!
FALSTAFF God-a-mercy! So should I be sure to be heart-burnt.

Enter HOSTESS

How now, dame Partlet the hen, have you enquired yet who   40
picked my pocket?
HOSTESS Why, Sir John, what do you think, Sir John, do you think I
keep thieves in my house? I have searched, I have enquired, so has
my husband, man by man, boy by boy, servant by servant – the
tithe of a hair was never lost in my house before.   45
FALSTAFF Ye lie, Hostess. Bardolph was shaved and lost many a hair,
and I'll be sworn my pocket was picked. Go to, you are a woman, go!
HOSTESS Who, I? No, I defy thee! God's light, I was never called so in
mine own house before.
FALSTAFF Go to, I know you well enough.   50
HOSTESS No, Sir John, you do not know me, Sir John. I know you, Sir
John. You owe me money, Sir John, and now you pick a quarrel
to beguile me of it. I bought you a dozen of shirts to your back.
FALSTAFF Dowlas, filthy dowlas. I have given them away to bakers'
wives. They have made bolters of them.   55
HOSTESS Now as I am a true woman, holland of eight shillings an ell!
You owe money here besides, Sir John, for your diet, and by-
drinkings, and money lent you, four-and-twenty pound.
FALSTAFF He had his part of it, let him pay.
HOSTESS He? Alas, he is poor, he hath nothing.   60
FALSTAFF How? Poor? Look upon his face. What call you rich? Let
them coin his nose, let them coin his cheeks, I'll not pay a denier.
What, will you make a younker of me? Shall I not take mine ease
in mine inn but I shall have my pocket picked? I have lost a seal-
ring of my grandfather's worth forty mark.   65
HOSTESS O Jesu, I have heard the Prince tell him I know not how oft,
that that ring was copper.

Falstaff's threat to beat Hal turns into a physical joke when the Prince appears. Falstaff again complains about being robbed, and insults the Hostess when she tells the truth.

1 Changing his tune

Falstaff threatens to beat ('cudgel') Hal for saying his seal-ring was copper, but when Hal enters immediately after the threat, Falstaff greets him in a quite different fashion. Invent some 'business' (stage action) for Falstaff, showing how he first uses his truncheon (a short heavy staff) in line 69 and then in the following stage direction.

2 '*Enter the* PRINCE *marching*'

Hal's appearance shows Falstaff that war is imminent. Turn the stage direction 'marching' into costume and movement suggestions for Hal.

3 Act out the comedy (in groups of four)

The episode between the Hostess, Bardolph, Hal and Falstaff is full of comic dialogue. Take parts and act out lines 68–144. In your first read-through, don't pause over expressions you don't understand. Remember that in the theatre, the audience does not get the chance to hold up the action to think about a particular meaning.

For example, no one today really knows why Shakespeare or his fellow Elizabethans found 'drawn fox' funny (line 91). Also, most people today think of Maid Marian (lines 91–2) as the virtuous girlfriend of Robin Hood. But in Shakespeare's time she was better known as a disreputable character in morris dances and May Day festivals. Falstaff says that compared with the Hostess, Maid Marian was as moral as the wife of a respectable town official ('deputy's wife of the ward').

As you prepare your performance, think of ways you can help the audience to find humour in such expressions.

Jack villain
sneak-up tell-tale
Is the wind in that door is that how things are
Newgate fashion like convicts in Newgate Prison going to be hanged

bonds contracts promising to pay money
stewed prune prostitute
drawn fox hunted fox

FALSTAFF How? The Prince is a Jack, a sneak-up. 'Sblood, an he were
here I would cudgel him like a dog if he would say so.

Enter the PRINCE *marching [with* PETO], *and Falstaff meets him,
playing upon his truncheon like a fife*

How now, lad? Is the wind in that door, i'faith, must we all march?   70
BARDOLPH Yea, two and two, Newgate fashion.
HOSTESS My lord, I pray you hear me.
PRINCE What sayest thou, Mistress Quickly? How doth thy husband?
I love him well, he is an honest man.
HOSTESS Good my lord, hear me.   75
FALSTAFF Prithee let her alone, and list to me.
PRINCE What sayest thou, Jack?
FALSTAFF The other night I fell asleep here, behind the arras, and had
my pocket picked. This house is turned bawdy-house, they pick
pockets.   80
PRINCE What didst thou lose, Jack?
FALSTAFF Wilt thou believe me, Hal, three or four bonds of forty
pound apiece, and a seal-ring of my grandfather's.
PRINCE A trifle, some eight-penny matter.
HOSTESS So I told him, my lord, and I said I heard your grace say so.   85
And, my lord, he speaks most vilely of you, like a foul-mouthed
man as he is, and said he would cudgel you.
PRINCE What! He did not?
HOSTESS There's neither faith, truth, nor womanhood in me else.
FALSTAFF There's no more faith in thee than in a stewed prune, nor no   90
more truth in thee than in a drawn fox – and for womanhood,
Maid Marian may be the deputy's wife of the ward to thee. Go,
you thing, go!
HOSTESS Say, what thing, what thing?
FALSTAFF What thing? Why, a thing to thank God on.   95
HOSTESS I am no thing to thank God on, I would thou shouldst know
it, I am an honest man's wife, and setting thy knighthood aside,
thou art a knave to call me so.
FALSTAFF Setting thy womanhood aside, thou art a beast to say
otherwise.   100
HOSTESS Say, what beast, thou knave, thou?

*The Hostess makes further accusations against Falstaff but he wriggles
out of each. Hal takes the Hostess' side and exposes Falstaff's lies.
Falstaff finds a way of making a joke of that!*

1 Sexual jokes (in pairs)

Lines 92–107 are full of *double entendres* (sexual double meanings). But
is the Hostess aware of the implications of what Falstaff and she herself
says? Experiment with different ways of speaking the lines to decide if
you think it is more appropriate to play her as knowing or not
understanding the sexual meanings of 'thing' (penis), 'beast' (over-
sexed animal) and 'have her' (have sex with her).

2 What tone?

In lines 126–35, Hal again insults Falstaff. Earlier, in the play-acting at
the tavern, under the pretence of playing his father, he had spoken in
the same style (Act 2 Scene 4, lines 369–80). Remind yourself of that
earlier condemnation, then speak Hal's lines opposite in the way you
would like to hear them on stage. Is he serious or joking?

3 Falstaff's methods

It is always dangerous to try to analyse comedy, because analysis can
kill humour stone dead. But use your experience of this scene to
suggest several strategies that Falstaff employs to deflect criticism and
to avoid facing reality.

Lines 136–9 contain an example of just one of Falstaff's verbal
tricks. Falstaff uses a biblical proverb ('all flesh is frail') to justify his
lies. He argues that because he has more flesh than other men, he has
more frailties: the fatter you are, the more likely you are to do wrong!

---

whelp cub
girdle belt
whoreson son of a prostitute
embossed frothing at mouth,
  swollen

reckonings bills
memorandums addresses
Adam in the Bible, the first man,
  who ate the apple of knowledge,
  and lost his innocence

FALSTAFF What beast? Why – an otter.

PRINCE An otter, Sir John? Why an otter?

FALSTAFF Why? She's neither fish nor flesh, a man knows not where
    to have her.   105

HOSTESS Thou art an unjust man in saying so, thou or any man knows
    where to have me, thou knave, thou.

PRINCE Thou sayest true, Hostess, and he slanders thee most grossly.

HOSTESS So he doth you, my lord, and said this other day you owed
    him a thousand pound.   110

PRINCE Sirrah, do I owe you a thousand pound?

FALSTAFF A thousand pound, Hal? A million, thy love is worth a
    million, thou owest me thy love.

HOSTESS Nay my lord, he called you Jack, and said he would cudgel
    you.   115

FALSTAFF Did I, Bardolph?

BARDOLPH Indeed, Sir John, you said so.

FALSTAFF Yea, if he said my ring was copper.

PRINCE I say 'tis copper, darest thou be as good as thy word now?

FALSTAFF Why Hal, thou knowest as thou art but man I dare, but as   120
    thou art prince, I fear thee as I fear the roaring of the lion's whelp.

PRINCE And why not as the lion?

FALSTAFF The King himself is to be feared as the lion. Dost thou think
    I'll fear thee as I fear thy father? Nay, an I do, I pray God my
    girdle break.   125

PRINCE O, if it should, how would thy guts fall about thy knees! But
    sirrah, there's no room for faith, truth, nor honesty in this bosom
    of thine. It is all filled up with guts and midriff. Charge an honest
    woman with picking thy pocket? Why, thou whoreson impudent
    embossed rascal, if there were anything in thy pocket but tavern   130
    reckonings, memorandums of bawdy-houses, and one poor
    pennyworth of sugar-candy to make thee long-winded, if thy
    pocket were enriched with any other injuries but these, I am a
    villain. And yet you will stand to it, you will not pocket up wrong!
    Art thou not ashamed?   135

FALSTAFF Dost thou hear, Hal? Thou knowest in the state of innocency
    Adam fell, and what should poor Jack Falstaff do in the days of
    villainy? Thou seest I have more flesh than another man, and
    therefore more frailty. You confess then, you picked my pocket?

Falstaff dismisses the Hostess as if he had done no wrong. Hal explains that the robbery money is repaid, he is friends with his father, and that Falstaff will command an infantry company in the coming war.

1 Chutzpah?

'Falstaff's four lines to the Hostess are chutzpah: sheer cheek!' Speak the lines aloud several times then say how far you agree with the 'chutzpah' judgement.

2 Always in character

Suggest how each of the following show that Falstaff is behaving true to form. Invent an accompanying action for each line that Falstaff might make to illustrate his meaning.

lines 151–2 'do it with unwashed hands too'

line 156 'O for a fine thief'

lines 157–8 'God be thanked for these rebels, they offend none but the virtuous'

lines 172–3 'Rare words! ... my drum'

3 The tone of command

Like his father at the end of Scene 2, Hal ends Scene 3 issuing commands and instructions for the coming war. Identify three or four ways in which lines 162–71 differ from Hal's 'Tavern language' (for example in lines 126–35).

4 Leaving – in style!

There are five separate exits opposite. Suggest the way each character leaves the stage in a style to fit his or her personality. Also say why you think Shakespeare packs four separate exits into the final twelve lines.

---

me tractable to I'll believe
pacified still my usual peaceful self
exchequer treasury
with unwashed hands without delay
procured obtained, granted

charge of foot company of infantry
heinously unprovided dreadfully ill-equipped
laud applaud
Temple hall Hall of the Inner Temple (one of the Inns of Court)

PRINCE It appears so by the story.   140

FALSTAFF Hostess, I forgive thee, go make ready breakfast, love thy
husband, look to thy servants, cherish thy guests, thou shalt find
me tractable to any honest reason, thou seest I am pacified still –
nay prithee be gone.

Exit Hostess

Now, Hal, to the news at court: for the robbery, lad, how is that   145
answered?

PRINCE O my sweet beef, I must still be good angel to thee – the
money is paid back again.

FALSTAFF O, I do not like that paying back, 'tis a double labour.

PRINCE I am good friends with my father and may do anything.   150

FALSTAFF Rob me the exchequer the first thing thou dost, and do it
with unwashed hands too.

BARDOLPH Do, my lord.

PRINCE I have procured thee, Jack, a charge of foot.

FALSTAFF I would it had been of horse. Where shall I find one that can   155
steal well? O for a fine thief of the age of two-and-twenty or
thereabouts! I am heinously unprovided. Well, God be thanked
for these rebels, they offend none but the virtuous. I laud them, I
praise them.

PRINCE Bardolph!   160

BARDOLPH My lord?

PRINCE Go bear this letter to Lord John of Lancaster,
  To my brother John, this to my Lord of Westmoreland.

[Exit Bardolph]

  Go, Peto, to horse, to horse, for thou and I
  Have thirty miles to ride yet ere dinner-time.   165

[Exit Peto]

  Jack, meet me tomorrow in the Temple hall
  At two o'clock in the afternoon.
  There shalt thou know thy charge, and there receive
  Money and order for their furniture.
  The land is burning, Percy stands on high,   170
  And either we or they must lower lie.   *[Exit]*

FALSTAFF Rare words! Brave world! Hostess, my breakfast, come!
  O, I could wish this tavern were my drum.   *[Exit]*

Looking back at Act 3
Activities for groups or individuals

1 Women in a man's world

The three women in the play never appear again after Act 3. Shakespeare portrays a relentlessly male world in which men have all the power, but have uneasy relationships with women. Falstaff exploits the Hostess; Hotspur seems dismissive of Kate; and Mortimer cannot speak his wife's language.

You have been invited to write a paragraph for a theatre programme for a production of the play. It has the title 'Women in a man's world'. Write your paragraph.

2 A soliloquy for King Henry?

Shakespeare often uses the sun as a symbol for kingship. For example, in Scene 2, line 79, King Henry speaks of 'sun-like majesty', and Hal at the end of Act 1 compares his time in the tavern with the sun being obscured by clouds.

Imagine a director wishes to open Scene 2 with Shakespeare's sonnet 33 spoken as a soliloquy by King Henry. Speak the sonnet aloud, then suggest how it might apply to the father–son relationship of Henry and Hal, and to other themes of the play.

> Full many a glorious morning have I seen
> Flatter the mountain tops with sovereign eye,
> Kissing with golden face the meadows green,
> Gilding pale streams with heavenly alchemy.
> Anon permit the basest clouds to ride
> With ugly rack on his celestial face,
> And from the forlorn world his visage hide,
> Stealing unseen to west with this disgrace.
> Even so my sun one early morn did shine
> With all triumphant splendour on my brow;
> But out alack! He was but one hour mine,
> The region cloud hath masked him from me now.
> > Yet him for this my love no whit disdaineth:
> > Suns of the world may stain, when heaven's sun staineth.

3 Hal's reformation

Scenes 2 and 3 portray further stages in Hal's reformation. He vows to
redeem himself by vanquishing Hotspur and taking over all his glory.
Design a costume for him in each scene. Your design should symbolise
Hal's gradual change towards the dignity he aims at.

4 Falstaff's seal-ring

If Falstaff did have a signet ring as he claims (but he may be lying),
what was it like? A seal-ring was used to 'sign' letters, and had a
personal emblem on it to signify some aspect of the owner. Think of a
likely sign for Falstaff, and design his seal-ring.

Hotspur and Kate. Use the questions on page 102 to help
you explore their relationship.

Hotspur praises Douglas as the world's greatest soldier. Douglas praises Hotspur in return. A messenger brings news that Northumberland is seriously ill and has been confined to bed for four days.

1 Soldiers exchange compliments (in pairs)

This is the first time Hotspur and Douglas appear together. They have fought each other three times in the past, but now are allies against King Henry. They praise each other extravagantly. Hotspur uses the image of stamping (minting) coins: Douglas' reputation ('attribution') is such that no soldier made this year ('this season's stamp') is so highly accepted by everyone ('go so general current'). Douglas' reply is equally flattering.

What did Douglas say just before the scene opens that prompts Hotspur to exclaim 'Well said, my noble Scot!' and to use such praise? Make up two to four lines for Douglas that precede line 1. Perhaps they may be about his previous meetings in battle with Hotspur.

2 The times

Hotspur calls the present times 'this fine age' (line 2), and 'a jostling time' (line 18). Check the interpretations suggested at the bottom of the page and think about what is in Hotspur's mind when he uses such descriptions. When you turn the page you will find Worcester immediately gives yet another description of the times.

3 The Messenger: courteous or ...? (in small groups)

This is the Messenger's only appearance in the play. Does he behave unusually for a servant or courtier speaking to the commander of the army? Suggest how Hotspur and Douglas react on hearing line 20, and use that line as your starting point for exploring how the Messenger might speak his six lines.

---

fine age hypocritical time
soothers flatterers
task me ... approve me put me to
 any test you like

potent powerful
beard defy, challenge
Zounds by God's wounds
jostling unquiet, turbulent
much feared by a great concern to

ACT 4 SCENE 1
Shrewsbury: the rebels' camp

Enter HOTSPUR, WORCESTER, *and* DOUGLAS

HOTSPUR Well said, my noble Scot! If speaking truth
         In this fine age were not thought flattery,
         Such attribution should the Douglas have
         As not a soldier of this season's stamp
         Should go so general current through the world.   5
         By God, I cannot flatter. I do defy
         The tongues of soothers, but a braver place
         In my heart's love hath no man than yourself.
         Nay, task me to my word, approve me, lord.
DOUGLAS Thou art the king of honour.   10
         No man so potent breathes upon the ground
         But I will beard him.
HOTSPUR   Do so, and 'tis well.

Enter MESSENGER *with letters*

         What letters hast thou there? – I can but thank you.
MESSENGER These letters come from your father.
HOTSPUR Letters from him? Why comes he not himself?   15
MESSENGER He cannot come, my lord, he is grievous sick.
HOTSPUR Zounds, how has he the leisure to be sick
         In such a jostling time? Who leads his power?
         Under whose government come they along?
MESSENGER His letters bear his mind, not I, my lord.   20
WORCESTER I prithee tell me, doth he keep his bed?
MESSENGER He did, my lord, four days ere I set forth,
         And at the time of my departure thence
         He was much feared by his physicians.

Northumberland's letter urges battle even though he himself is sick.
Hotspur and Douglas comfort themselves with the thought that even if
they lose the first battle, Northumberland's army is in reserve.

1 A break in reading

Hotspur breaks off in the middle of reading the letter from his father.
His unfinished sentence at line 31 reports that Northumberland is sick.
The next sentence moves to a new topic: that Northumberland's
deputies cannot quickly gather together ('drawn') an army, nor did he
think it appropriate ('meet') that anyone other than himself ('any soul
removed') should bear that responsibility.

Advise the actor playing Hotspur what stage business he could use
to move from line 31 to line 32 so that the audience understands why
he stops in mid-sentence.

2 Good out of bad (in pairs)

Northumberland's failure to arrive with an army is a serious blow to
the rebels' cause. But Hotspur finds comfort in an image from gambling.
Northumberland's absence ('present want') means that they are not
risking everything on a single throw of the dice ('All at one cast'). It is
not wise in such a risky enterprise ('nice hazard') to chance everything
in the outcome of a single battle.

Everything in lines 44–59 is on the theme of finding something good
about Northumberland's absence. Take parts and speak the lines to
each other in the mood of two men desperately concerned to cheer each
other up and to find comfort in an unlucky circumstance.

Afterwards, talk together about whether you think both men really
believe what they are saying, or are simply trying to keep their spirits up.

---

whole healthy
advertisement instruction
conjunction combined armies
quailing shrinking back
purposes intentions
main prize, army

very bottom ... soul ... list ...
  bound absolute total
sweet reversion future wealth
  ahead
comfort of retirement security to
  fall back on
  maidenhead beginning

WORCESTER I would the state of time had first been whole   25
          Ere he by sickness had been visited.
          His health was never better worth than now.
HOTSPUR Sick now? Droop now? This sickness doth infect
          The very life-blood of our enterprise.
          'Tis catching hither, even to our camp.   30
          He writes me here that inward sickness –
          And that his friends by deputation could not
          So soon be drawn, nor did he think it meet
          To lay so dangerous and dear a trust
          On any soul removed but on his own.   35
          Yet doth he give us bold advertisement
          That with our small conjunction we should on,
          To see how fortune is disposed to us.
          For, as he writes, there is no quailing now,
          Because the King is certainly possessed   40
          Of all our purposes. What say you to it?
WORCESTER Your father's sickness is a maim to us.
HOTSPUR A perilous gash, a very limb lopped off –
          And yet, in faith, it is not! His present want
          Seems more than we shall find it. Were it good   45
          To set the exact wealth of all our states
          All at one cast? To set so rich a main
          On the nice hazard of one doubtful hour?
          It were not good, for therein should we read
          The very bottom and the soul of hope,   50
          The very list, the very utmost bound
          Of all our fortunes.
DOUGLAS Faith, and so we should. Where now remains
          A sweet reversion – we may boldly spend
          Upon the hope of what is to come in.   55
          A comfort of retirement lives in this.
HOTSPUR A rendezvous, a home to fly unto,
          If that the devil and mischance look big
          Upon the maidenhead of our affairs.

*Worcester fears that Northumberland's absence will make people question
the rebel cause. Hotspur argues that a small army gains greater glory
and reputation. News arrives of Henry's approach.*

1 Worcester the politician (in pairs)

In contrast with Hotspur's reckless optimism, Worcester is cautious.
He is all too aware of the danger the rebels are in because of
Northumberland's absence. Like many politicians he wants to avoid
any close scrutiny ('strict arbitrement'). He therefore urges that the
rebels block any enquiry into their affairs, ensuring there are no
viewing points or loopholes ('stop all sight-holes, every loop'). If
people know of Northumberland's absence, they will fear the worst.

Speak Worcester's lines as persuasively as you can. Give emphasis to
every word or phrase that contributes to the force of his argument.
Afterwards, talk together about whether you think Worcester's argument
is sound common sense or untrustworthy political pleading.

2 Hot-headed or hesitating? (in small groups)

Explore the different interpretations of Hotspur's character that pausing
or not pausing could suggest:

a How quickly does Hotspur reject Worcester's argument? Advise
the actor whether he should instantly speak 'You strain too far' at
line 75, or whether he might pause for some time before
responding.

b How quickly does Hotspur speak 'No harm' (line 90) and 'He
shall be welcome too' (line 94) when he learns of the size of the
armies coming to attack him?

---

quality and hair very nature
Brooks tolerates, permits
apprehension thought,
 interpretation
fearful faction frightened
 supporters
off'ring side rebel cause

aloof distant
strain too far over-imagine, are
 too fearful
make a head/To push recruit an
 army to fight
joints limbs

WORCESTER But yet I would your father had been here.   60
        The quality and hair of our attempt
        Brooks no division. It will be thought,
        By some that know not why he is away,
        That wisdom, loyalty, and mere dislike
        Of our proceedings kept the Earl from hence.   65
        And think how such an apprehension
        May turn the tide of fearful faction,
        And breed a kind of question in our cause.
        For well you know we of the off'ring side
        Must keep aloof from strict arbitrement,   70
        And stop all sight-holes, every loop from whence
        The eye of reason may pry in upon us.
        This absence of your father's draws a curtain
        That shows the ignorant a kind of fear
        Before not dreamt of.
HOTSPUR   You strain too far.   75
        I rather of his absence make this use.
        It lends a lustre and more great opinion,
        A larger dare to our great enterprise,
        Than if the Earl were here. For men must think
        If we without his help can make a head   80
        To push against a kingdom, with his help
        We shall o'erturn it topsy-turvy down.
        Yet all goes well, yet all our joints are whole.
DOUGLAS As heart can think. There is not such a word
        Spoke of in Scotland as this term of fear.   85

Enter SIR RICHARD VERNON

HOTSPUR My cousin Vernon! Welcome, by my soul!
VERNON Pray God my news be worth a welcome, lord.
        The Earl of Westmoreland seven thousand strong
        Is marching hitherwards, with him Prince John.
HOTSPUR No harm, what more?
VERNON   And further, I have learned,   90
        The King himself in person is set forth,
        Or hitherwards intended speedily,
        With strong and mighty preparation.

Vernon paints a dazzling picture of Hal and his knights, splendidly armed for battle, the image of chivalry and legend. Hotspur looks forward to slaughtering them all and killing Hal in personal combat.

1 An image of chivalry

Vernon was deeply impressed by the magnificent spectacle of the power of medieval chivalry on display, and he delivers a glittering, heroic description of Hal and his knights.

a Rehearse speaking Vernon's lines to greatest dramatic effect.

b There are ten images in Vernon's description. Identify each, then choose one or two to illustrate in a drawing or design. To help you:

'plumed like estridges' (line 98) – the Prince of Wales' symbol is a plume of ostrich feathers. The knights wear them on their helmets.

'In golden coats like images' (line 100) – Hal's knights wear surcoats over their armour: sleeveless loose fitting tunics, each bearing a coat of arms.

'feathered Mercury' (line 106) – in Roman mythology, the gods' messenger (with winged heels)

2 Blood and fire (in pairs)

Hotspur reacts passionately to Vernon's glowing praise of Hal, implying it makes him sick ('agues'). His language is ominous and threatening. He imagines Hal's soldiers as sacrifices on the bloody altar of 'the fire-eyed maid' (Bellona, goddess of war) and 'The mailèd Mars' (the armoured god of war).

As one person speaks Hotspur's lines 111–24, the other echoes every 'negative' aggressive or threatening word.

daft wave, dismiss	**Pegasus** (in Greek mythology)
furnished ready for battle	a flying horse
Bated beat their wings, refreshed	**witch** bewitch
beaver face guard of helmet	**trim** ceremonial costume
cushes thigh armour	**reprisal** prize, booty
seat saddle	**nigh** near

HOTSPUR He shall be welcome too. Where is his son
     The nimble-footed madcap Prince of Wales,   95
     And his comrades that daft the world aside
     And bid it pass?
VERNON   All furnished, all in arms,
     All plumed like estridges that with the wind
     Bated, like eagles having lately bath'd,
     Glittering in golden coats like images,   100
     As full of spirit as the month of May,
     And gorgeous as the sun at midsummer,
     Wanton as youthful goats, wild as young bulls.
     I saw young Harry with his beaver on,
     His cushes on his thighs, gallantly armed,   105
     Rise from the ground like feathered Mercury,
     And vaulted with such ease into his seat
     As if an angel dropped down from the clouds
     To turn and wind a fiery Pegasus,
     And witch the world with noble horsemanship. 110
HOTSPUR No more, no more! Worse than the sun in March,
     This praise doth nourish agues. Let them come!
     They come like sacrifices in their trim,
     And to the fire-eyed maid of smoky war
     All hot and bleeding will we offer them.   115
     The mailèd Mars shall on his altar sit
     Up to the ears in blood. I am on fire
     To hear this rich reprisal is so nigh,
     And yet not ours! Come, let me taste my horse,
     Who is to bear me like a thunderbolt   120
     Against the bosom of the Prince of Wales.
     Harry to Harry shall, hot horse to horse,
     Meet and ne'er part till one drop down a corpse.
     O that Glendower were come!

Vernon reports that Glendower's army is not yet ready. Hotspur prepares for battle, mocking at death. Scene 2 finds Falstaff marching towards Coventry, and still thinking of drink and money.

---

1 'Doomsday is near'

Vernon's news depresses Douglas and Worcester, but Hotspur is defiant and hopes to gain victory even with a smaller army. He and Douglas each speak a final rhyming couplet.

Suggest the way in which each of the four characters leave the stage. Use their language opposite to guide you. Their movements, expressions and gestures should show the audience what each man thinks lies in store for him in the coming battle.

2 The road to Shrewsbury

Turn to the map on page 2 to identify the locations of Scene 2. Make your own copy of Falstaff's campaign map to show his route from London to Shrewsbury. It is likely to show the taverns along the way (see lines 38–9).

3 Making a pun (in pairs)

Falstaff can rarely resist a pun, especially if it gets him out of trouble. In line 6, Bardolph reminds him that the bottle of sack will cost ('makes') an angel: a coin worth one third of £1. But Falstaff deliberately misunderstands 'makes' and replies as if Bardolph can make money out of the bottle! Falstaff even offers to ensure that any profit that Bardolph makes will be in real money ('I'll answer the coinage').

Work out some stage business which can help an audience understand the humour of lines 1–10 without killing the enjoyment!

---

draw his power collect together his army

tidings news

whole battle total number of soldiers

muster roll-call, assembly of the army

Lay out use your own money

coinage quality of the money

VERNON   There is more news.
    I learned in Worcester as I rode along   125
    He cannot draw his power this fourteen days.
DOUGLAS That's the worst tidings that I hear of yet.
WORCESTER Ay, by my faith, that bears a frosty sound.
HOTSPUR What may the King's whole battle reach unto?
VERNON To thirty thousand.
HOTSPUR   Forty let it be.   130
    My father and Glendower being both away,
    The powers of us may serve so great a day.
    Come, let us take a muster speedily.
    Doomsday is near. Die all, die merrily.
DOUGLAS Talk not of dying, I am out of fear   135
    Of death or death's hand for this one half year.

Exeunt

ACT 4   SCENE 2
A road near Coventry

Enter FALSTAFF and BARDOLPH

FALSTAFF Bardolph, get thee before to Coventry. Fill me a bottle of
    sack. Our soldiers shall march through. We'll to Sutton Coldfield
    tonight.
BARDOLPH Will you give me money, captain?
FALSTAFF Lay out, lay out.   5
BARDOLPH This bottle makes an angel.
FALSTAFF And if it do, take it for thy labour – and if it make twenty,
    take them all, I'll answer the coinage. Bid my lieutenant Peto meet
    me at town's end.
BARDOLPH I will, captain. Farewell.   10

Exit

Falstaff tells of the corrupt recruiting methods he used to make money.
He took bribes from well-off recruits and filled their places with down-
and-outs and prisoners. They are a wretched sight.

1 Making money out of soldiers (in small groups)

Falstaff's description of his soldiers is in stark contrast to Vernon's picture of Hal's knights on page 133. Shakespeare's audience would be very familiar with Falstaff's corrupt recruiting methods. 'The King's press' was much in use in the 1590s to conscript soldiers for various military expeditions. Officers were allowed to press-gang soldiers against their will.

Some of Falstaff's recruits have 'bought out their services' by paying him a bribe: the 'good householders' and 'yeomen's sons', the men about to get married, whose banns (announcement of marriage) had been called in church, the milksops and cowards ('warm slaves', 'toasts-and-butter').

In their place, Falstaff has recruited the underclass of society: sacked servants, prisoners, runaway barmen ('revolted tapsters'), out-of-work stablemen ('ostlers trade-fallen'), and men with no hope of inheriting any money or land ('younger sons to younger brothers': only first-born sons could inherit).

Falstaff uses two images from the Bible to describe his recruits. Lazarus (line 22) was poor and sickly, mistreated by the rich man's dogs (the rich man is Dives, who Falstaff mentions at Act 3 Scene 3, line 24). Lines 29–30 echo the parable of the Prodigal Son whose job was looking after pigs and who ate pigswill ('draff and husks').

a Explore ways of speaking Falstaff's soliloquy. Should some soldiers from Falstaff's company be on stage to show their condition? Which lines might Falstaff speak directly to them?

b See page 150 for an activity on recruiting.

---

soused gurnet small pickled fish	**fazed ancient** frayed flag
as lief rather	**gibbets** gallows
caliver small musket	**gyves** shackles on legs
struck fowl wounded bird	**linen ... hedge** washing placed to
ancients ensigns, standard bearers	dry on hedge
painted cloth cheap wall hanging	**quilt** padded jacket (called a Jack)

FALSTAFF If I be not ashamed of my soldiers, I am a soused gurnet. I have misused the King's press damnably. I have got in exchange of a hundred-and-fifty soldiers three hundred and odd pounds. I press me none but good householders, yeomen's sons, enquire me out contracted bachelors, such as had been asked twice on the banns, 15 such a commodity of warm slaves as had as lief hear the devil as a drum, such as fear the report of a caliver worse than a struck fowl or a hurt wild duck. I pressed me none but such toasts-and-butter, with hearts in their bellies no bigger than pins' heads, and they have bought out their services. And now my whole charge consists of 20 ancients, corporals, lieutenants, gentlemen of companies – slaves as ragged as Lazarus in the painted cloth, where the glutton's dogs licked his sores. And such as indeed were never soldiers, but discarded unjust serving-men, younger sons to younger brothers, revolted tapsters, and ostlers trade-fallen, the cankers of a calm 25 world and a long peace, ten times more dishonourable-ragged than an old fazed ancient. And such have I to fill up the rooms of them as have bought out their services, that you would think that I had a hundred-and-fifty tattered prodigals lately come from swine-keeping, from eating draff and husks. A mad fellow met me on the 30 way, and told me I had unloaded all the gibbets and pressed the dead bodies. No eye hath seen such scarecrows. I'll not march through Coventry with them, that's flat. Nay, and the villains march wide betwixt the legs as if they had gyves on, for indeed I had the most of them out of prison. There's not a shirt and a half in all my company, 35 and the half shirt is two napkins tacked together and thrown over the shoulders like a herald's coat without sleeves. And the shirt, to say the truth, stolen from my host at Saint Albans, or the red-nose innkeeper of Daventry. But that's all one, they'll find linen enough on every hedge. 40

Enter the PRINCE, [*and the*] LORD OF WESTMORELAND

PRINCE How now, blown Jack? How now, quilt?

Falstaff greets Hal and Westmoreland, implying he is ready for action. He describes his soldiers as mere cannon-fodder, and leaves hoping more for food than for battle.

1 'Food for powder' (in small groups)

Falstaff dismisses Hal's remark on the pitiful appearance of his soldiers. In lines 54–6, he cynically comments that his troops are good enough to toss on the end of pikes, are merely cannon-fodder, and will fill up graves as well as better men.

a How do the lines affect your view of Falstaff's character?

b Imagine you have joined a team making a film on the horrors of war. You have been given a special commission to create a one-minute sequence of images for which Falstaff's words are used as voice-over. Design a story-board: sketches of each frame of your sequence illustrating or listing the images and script.

c Contrast the lines with Vernon's description of Hal and his knights in the previous scene (lines 97–110). As one person speaks Vernon's lines, the other punctuates them with extracts from Falstaff's comments on his own soldiers.

2 Food rather than fighting

As Falstaff leaves the stage, he speaks a rhyming couplet (in Shakespeare's time, 'feast' and 'guest' could rhyme). It is his version of an old proverb: cowards prefer to turn up at the end of a fight and the beginning of a banquet.

Just how does Falstaff exit to show what he thinks of taking part in the coming battle? In one production, he winked broadly at the audience, and placed his finger knowingly alongside his nose. Make your own suggestions.

---

cry you mercy beg your pardon
powers forces, army
toss throw into battle, pitch on the end of a pike

three fingers in the ribs fat (a 'finger' was a measurement of three-quarters of an inch)
in the field ready for battle
fray fight

FALSTAFF What, Hal! How now, mad wag? What a devil dost thou in
     Warwickshire? My good Lord of Westmoreland, I cry you mercy,
     I thought your honour had already been at Shrewsbury.

WESTMORELAND Faith, Sir John, 'tis more than time that I were   45
     there, and you too, but my powers are there already. The King I
     can tell you looks for us all, we must away all night.

FALSTAFF Tut, never fear me, I am as vigilant as a cat to steal cream.

PRINCE I think, to steal cream indeed, for thy theft hath already made
     thee butter. But tell me, Jack, whose fellows are these that come   50
     after?

FALSTAFF Mine, Hal, mine.

PRINCE I did never see such pitiful rascals.

FALSTAFF Tut, tut, good enough to toss, food for powder, food for
     powder, they'll fill a pit as well as better. Tush, man, mortal men,   55
     mortal men.

WESTMORELAND Ay, but Sir John, methinks they are exceeding poor
     and bare, too beggarly.

FALSTAFF Faith, for their poverty I know not where they had that.
     And for their bareness I am sure they never learned that of me.   60

PRINCE No, I'll be sworn, unless you call three fingers in the ribs bare.
     But sirrah, make haste. Percy is already in the field.

                                                                Exit

FALSTAFF What, is the King encamped?

WESTMORELAND He is, Sir John, I fear we shall stay too long.

                                                                [*Exit*]

FALSTAFF Well,   65
     To the latter end of a fray, and the beginning of a feast
     Fits a dull fighter and a keen guest.

                                                                [*Exit*]

Hotspur and Douglas urge immediate battle against King Henry, but Vernon and Worcester advise caution. Vernon resents Douglas' accusation of cowardice, and explains that the cavalry need rest.

1 Quarrels in the camp (in groups of four)

The rebels' argument about the most suitable course of action shows that relationships are very strained. Take parts and enact lines 1–29, bearing the following points in mind:

- How can you speak the short clipped speeches to convey a sense of tension before the coming battle? Experiment to test the theatrical convention that when a line is shared, there is no pause between speakers.
- How close to physical action against each other do Vernon and Douglas get in lines 6–14?
- What tone does Vernon use as he explains his reasons for delay in lines 16–24: sarcastic, or friendly and reasonable, or ...?
- Do they stand or sit, move or stay still? Work out how to show the opposing views in their physical relationships on stage (Hotspur and Douglas versus Worcester and Vernon).

2 Design tasks: set and props

Imagine you are the designer of a production. You have been asked to design two versions of the set and props for this scene in the rebels' camp for two very different stagings:

- on a bare stage with the very minimum of props.
- in a very elaborate production that will try to recreate the camp as realistically as possible.

whit bit	**leading** military experience
supply reinforcements	**impediments** drawbacks
counsel (line 6) advise	**horse** cavalry
counsel (line 11) conversation	**pride and mettle** courageous spirit

ACT 4 SCENE 3
Shrewsbury: the rebels' camp

Enter HOTSPUR, WORCESTER, DOUGLAS, *and* VERNON

HOTSPUR We'll fight with him tonight.
WORCESTER   It may not be.
DOUGLAS You give him then advantage.
VERNON   Not a whit.
HOTSPUR Why say you so, looks he not for supply?
VERNON So do we.
HOTSPUR   His is certain, ours is doubtful.
WORCESTER Good cousin, be advised, stir not tonight.   5
VERNON Do not, my lord.
DOUGLAS   You do not counsel well.
    You speak it out of fear and cold heart.
VERNON Do me no slander, Douglas. By my life,
    And I dare well maintain it with my life,
    If well-respected honour bid me on,   10
    I hold as little counsel with weak fear
    As you, my lord, or any Scot that this day lives.
    Let it be seen tomorrow in the battle
    Which of us fears.
DOUGLAS   Yea, or tonight.
VERNON   Content.
HOTSPUR Tonight, say I.   15
VERNON Come, come, it may not be. I wonder much,
    Being men of such great leading as you are,
    That you foresee not what impediments
    Drag back our expedition. Certain horse
    Of my cousin Vernon's are not yet come up,   20
    Your uncle Worcester's horse came but today,
    And now their pride and mettle is asleep,
    Their courage with hard labour tame and dull,
    That not a horse is half the half of himself.

Worcester argues that their forces are outnumbered. Hotspur praises
Blunt who brings a message: King Henry is ready to grant all Hotspur's
wishes and pardon all the rebels. Hotspur begins his story.

'Welcome, Sir Walter Blunt.' From left to right: Blunt, Worcester, Hotspur.

1 Hotspur's grievances

The historical information on page 1 provides the background to the
story which Hotspur tells from line 54. He claims that the Percy family
put Henry on the throne, welcoming him when he had few supporters
and was very unpopular ('Sick in the world's regard'). He uses loaded
words like 'sneaking home' to describe Henry's return to England.

You will find an activity on Hotspur's story on page 144.

journey-bated travel-weary	**charge** mission, purpose
parley conference	**conjure** bring out
of our determination on our side	**good deserts** merits, good deeds
quality party, cause	**manifold** many
out of limit beyond all boundaries	**with interest** to the full
anointed majesty the true king	**unminded** insignificant

HOTSPUR So are the horses of the enemy   25
        In general journey-bated and brought low.
        The better part of ours are full of rest.
WORCESTER The number of the King exceedeth ours.
        For God's sake, cousin, stay till all come in.
        The trumpet sounds a parley

        Enter SIR WALTER BLUNT

BLUNT I come with gracious offers from the King,   30
        If you vouchsafe me hearing and respect.
HOTSPUR Welcome, Sir Walter Blunt: and would to God
        You were of our determination!
        Some of us love you well, and even those some
        Envy your great deservings and good name,   35
        Because you are not of our quality,
        But stand against us like an enemy.
BLUNT And God defend but still I should stand so,
        So long as out of limit and true rule
        You stand against anointed majesty.   40
        But to my charge. The King hath sent to know
        The nature of your griefs, and whereupon
        You conjure from the breast of civil peace
        Such bold hostility, teaching his duteous land
        Audacious cruelty. If that the King   45
        Have any way your good deserts forgot,
        Which he confesseth to be manifold,
        He bids you name your griefs, and with all speed
        You shall have your desires with interest
        And pardon absolute for yourself, and these   50
        Herein misled by your suggestion.
HOTSPUR The King is kind, and well we know the King
        Knows at what time to promise, when to pay.
        My father, and my uncle, and myself
        Did give him that same royalty he wears,   55
        And when he was not six-and-twenty strong,
        Sick in the world's regard, wretched and low,
        A poor unminded outlaw sneaking home,
        My father gave him welcome to the shore.

Hotspur lists the rebels' grievances against King Henry: the support of the Percies rallied everyone to his cause, but he became over-ambitious, deposing King Richard and refusing to help Mortimer.

1 Act out Hotspur's story (whole class)

Hotspur's long catalogue of grievances against King Henry can be seen as his summary of two Shakespeare plays, *Richard II* and this one. Lines 54–92 recapitulate, from Hotspur's point of view, many of the events in *Richard II*. Lines 93–105 are a selective summary of events in *Henry IV Part 1*.

An actor playing Hotspur must find a suitable way in which to deliver the lines: how much anger and emphasis, where he pauses, where he varies the pace of speaking, what accompanying gestures.

Work out a way of performing Hotspur's story. As there are well over thirty distinct events in Hotspur's story, the lines can be shared among three groups (lines 54–73, 74–92 and 93–105). Each group enacts its part of the story.

The following explanations can help your preparation:

'sue his livery' (line 62) – legally regain his ducal lands

'terms of zeal' (line 63) – vows of loyalty to the king

'lean to him' (line 67) – support Bullingbrook (King Henry)

'more and less' (line 68) – people of every social class

'cap and knee' (line 68) – bareheaded and kneeling

'proffered him their oaths' (line 71) – swore allegiance to him

'Gave him their heirs as pages' (line 72) – offered their sons to attend him

After your performances, work in pairs and speak the whole story to each other as it might be delivered on stage.

---

while his blood was poor before he claimed to be royal

edicts ... decrees harsh laws

seeming brow hypocritical appearance

angle for use bribes to catch

personal personally fighting

in the neck of that immediately after

tasked taxed

March (that is, Mortimer)

were well placed had their own property

engaged held prisoner

And when he heard him swear and vow to God 60
He came but to be Duke of Lancaster,
To sue his livery, and beg his peace
With tears of innocency and terms of zeal,
My father, in kind heart and pity moved,
Swore him assistance, and performed it too. 65
Now, when the lords and barons of the realm
Perceived Northumberland did lean to him,
The more and less came in with cap and knee,
Met him in boroughs, cities, villages,
Attended him on bridges, stood in lanes, 70
Laid gifts before him, proffered him their oaths,
Gave him their heirs as pages, followed him
Even at the heels in golden multitudes.
He presently, as greatness knows itself,
Steps me a little higher than his vow 75
Made to my father while his blood was poor
Upon the naked shore at Ravenspurgh;
And now forsooth takes on him to reform
Some certain edicts and some strait decrees
That lie too heavy on the commonwealth, 80
Cries out upon abuses, seems to weep
Over his country's wrongs – and by this face,
This seeming brow of justice, did he win
The hearts of all that he did angle for.
Proceeded further – cut me off the heads 85
Of all the favourites that the absent King
In deputation left behind him here,
When he was personal in the Irish war.

BLUNT Tut, I came not to hear this.

HOTSPUR   Then to the point.
In short time after he deposed the King, 90
Soon after that deprived him of his life,
And in the neck of that tasked the whole state.
To make that worse, suffered his kinsman March –
Who is, if every owner were well placed,
Indeed his King – to be engaged in Wales, 95
There without ransom to lie forfeited.

Hotspur's long list of grievances ends with the claim that Henry's right to the throne is dubious. Hotspur asks for more time to consider. In Scene 4, the Archbishop dispatches messages to Henry's enemies.

1 A final grievance

Several of Hotspur's complaints have occurred earlier in the play: Henry's refusal to ransom Mortimer, and Worcester's and Northumberland's dismissal from Henry's Council and court. Other grievances are not shown: the activities of spies ('intelligence'), and Henry breaking many vows and committing many wrongs (line 101).

Hotspur ends his long list of complaints by saying that the rebels have investigated Henry's right to be king, and found his title 'Too indirect' to last long.

Turn to page 1 to remind yourself of the family tree of England's royal family. Then imagine yourself as a lawyer commissioned by the Percy family to write a brief and clear account of whether Henry has a legal right to the throne. Write your report.

2 Out of character?

Hotspur proposes that Worcester visit the king tomorrow morning to report what the rebels have finally decided. His final line seems to offer the prospect of peace. Suggest some reasons why Hotspur, who up to this point seemed hot-headed and impetuous, now offers hope of avoiding battle.

3 Two new characters (in pairs)

Scene 4 introduces two new characters who do not appear again in the play. The Archbishop of York is an enemy of the king and is plotting a further rebellion which will occur in *Henry IV Part 2*. Take parts and speak the scene, then try some of the activities on page 148.

Rated scolded, berated
head of safety army for self defence
withal also
pry/Into his title examine Henry's claim to the throne
impawned pledged

Hie make haste
sealèd brief secret letter
the Lord Marshal Thomas Mowbray, Duke of Norfolk, who appears in *Henry IV Part 2* as a leader of a further rebellion
tenor meaning

Disgraced me in my happy victories,
Sought to entrap me by intelligence,
Rated mine uncle from the Council-board,
In rage dismissed my father from the court, 100
Broke oath on oath, committed wrong on wrong,
And in conclusion drove us to seek out
This head of safety, and withal to pry
Into his title, the which we find
Too indirect for long continuance. 105

BLUNT Shall I return this answer to the King?

HOTSPUR Not so, Sir Walter. We'll withdraw a while.
Go to the King, and let there be impawned
Some surety for a safe return again,
And in the morning early shall mine uncle 110
Bring him our purposes – and so, farewell.

BLUNT I would you would accept of grace and love.

HOTSPUR And may be so we shall.

BLUNT   Pray God you do.   [*Exeunt*]

ACT 4   SCENE 4
York: the Archbishop's palace

Enter the ARCHBISHOP OF YORK and SIR MICHAEL

ARCHBISHOP Hie, good Sir Michael, bear this sealèd brief
With wingèd haste to the Lord Marshal,
This to my cousin Scroop, and all the rest
To whom they are directed. If you knew
How much they do import, you would make haste. 5

SIR MICHAEL My good lord,
I guess their tenor.

The Archbishop fears that Hotspur's army, weakened by absence, will lose the coming battle. He also fears that King Henry will then attack him, and so lays plans to recruit another rebel army.

1 Who is Sir Michael?

No one knows if a real-life Sir Michael existed, because he does not appear in any historical record. He speaks only eight lines, then disappears for ever. If you were chosen to act the part of Sir Michael, how would you prepare for the role?

2 Shakespeare looks ahead?

Scene 4 looks forward to the second part of *Henry IV*, in which the Archbishop plays a major role in another rebellion against King Henry. The scene is often used in arguments that Shakespeare planned *Henry IV Parts 1* and *2* as one play, but split it in two because it was too long to stage as a single play.

Scene 4 is often cut in performance by those who claim that it does not advance the action of the play. But other productions keep it in, arguing that it is dramatically effective in creating an atmosphere of foreboding about the outcome of the battle of Shrewsbury.

Give reasons for whether or not you would cut the whole scene if you were directing the play.

3 Understatement

'He means to visit us' says the Archbishop in line 37, about King Henry's intention after defeating Hotspur. What kind of a visit does the Archbishop have in mind?

---

bide the touch be put to the test (as gold is tested with a touchstone)
Lord Harry (that is, Hotspur)
power was in the first proportion army was the largest
rated sinew valued source of strength

instant trial immediate battle
special head best soldiers
corrivals partners, allies
confederacy links with the rebels
make strong recruit an army

ARCHBISHOP   Like enough you do.
          Tomorrow, good Sir Michael, is a day
          Wherein the fortune of ten thousand men
          Must bide the touch. For, sir, at Shrewsbury,   10
          As I am truly given to understand,
          The King with mighty and quick-raisèd power
          Meets with Lord Harry, and I fear, Sir Michael,
          What with the sickness of Northumberland,
          Whose power was in the first proportion,   15
          And what with Owen Glendower's absence thence,
          Who with them was a rated sinew too,
          And comes not in, o'er-ruled by prophecies,
          I fear the power of Percy is too weak
          To wage an instant trial with the King.   20
SIR MICHAEL Why, my good lord, you need not fear,
          There is Douglas, and Lord Mortimer.
ARCHBISHOP No, Mortimer is not there.
SIR MICHAEL But there is Mordake, Vernon, Lord Harry Percy,
          And there is my Lord of Worcester, and a head   25
          Of gallant warriors, noble gentlemen.
ARCHBISHOP And so there is. But yet the King hath drawn
          The special head of all the land together.
          The Prince of Wales, Lord John of Lancaster,
          The noble Westmoreland, and warlike Blunt,   30
          And many more corrivals and dear men
          Of estimation and command in arms.
SIR MICHAEL Doubt not, my lord, they shall be well opposed.
ARCHBISHOP I hope no less, yet needful 'tis to fear,
          And to prevent the worst, Sir Michael, speed.   35
          For if Lord Percy thrive not, ere the King
          Dismiss his power he means to visit us,
          For he hath heard of our confederacy,
          And 'tis but wisdom to make strong against him.
          Therefore make haste – I must go write again   40
          To other friends. And so, farewell, Sir Michael.

                                        Exeunt

Looking back at Act 4
Activities for groups or individuals

1 Dramatic construction

As happens throughout the play, each scene in Act 4 contains ironic and dramatic contrasts with its neighbouring scenes. Scene 1 ends with the heroic language of Hotspur and Douglas, immediately followed by Scene 2 opening with Falstaff's concern for a drink. Scene 2 closes with Falstaff wanting to arrive after a battle has ended, and Scene 3 opens with Hotspur's 'We'll fight with him tonight'. Scene 3 ends with a faint hope of peace, but Scene 4 opens with another planned rebellion.

Prepare a series of tableaux based on the endings and beginnings of scenes to show their contrasting attitudes and moods.

2 Falstaff's recruits

Find a copy of *Henry IV Part 2* and read Act 3 Scene 2. It shows just how Falstaff goes about recruiting a similar company of very unsuitable soldiers to those described in Scene 2. Afterwards, improvise your own recruiting scene as Falstaff chooses his recruits.

3 Promise keeping

Most of the major characters in the play have promises to keep. Step into role as each in turn (King Henry, Hal, Falstaff, Worcester, Hotspur, Northumberland). State an important promise you propose to keep and why (for example, King Henry plans a Crusade to redeem his sin in seizing Richard II's crown). Which promises have been kept so far?

4 Order and disorder

The theme of order breaking down continues in Act 4. For example, in Scene 1 Hotspur vows destruction of King Henry's army (lines 111–23). Identify two or three examples of the theme in each scene.

5 'In golden coats like images'

Remind yourself of Vernon's dazzling description of Hal and his knights (Scene 1, lines 97–110). Then design the surcoats of Prince Hal and several of his knights.

'Doomsday is near. Die all, die merrily.'
How closely does this illustration match your view of Hotspur?

King Henry and Hal comment on nature's ominous signs that foretell disorder. Henry rebukes Worcester for causing conflict and asks him to restore order. Worcester claims he has not sought the coming battle.

1 Nature and society

Dawn breaks over Shrewsbury, but the signs are ominous. Shakespeare, like many of his fellow Elizabethans, enjoyed making comparisons between nature and society. They often claimed that disorder in nature (like a tempest) reflected and predicted turmoil in human affairs and disorder in the state (like the overthrow of a king).

Identify the imagery in lines 1–6 and 17–21 which makes such links between nature and society. To help you:

lines 1–6 use personification: turning non-human things into persons, giving them human feelings and attributes.

lines 17–21: many Elizabethans believed that the Earth was at the centre of the universe, and that all other planets orbited around it in perfect order.

2 More imagery

Use the help provided on page 197 to identify other uses of imagery on the opposite page (for example, in lines 12, 13, 15–16, 24 and 25).

3 History into drama

King Henry talks about his 'old limbs' (line 13). But at the battle of Shrewsbury the historical King Henry was just 37 years old, Hotspur was 40 and Prince Hal only 17. For Shakespeare's alteration of history to suit his dramatic purposes, see page 200.

---

his distemperature the sun's sickness
doff remove
ungentle steel armour
all-abhorrèd all-hated
obedient orb dutiful orbit

exhal'd meteor shooting star (a menacing omen)
prodigy of fear fearful omen
broachèd mischief full-flowing rebellion
unborn times future
lag end final few years

ACT 5 SCENE 1
Shrewsbury: King Henry's camp

Enter the KING, PRINCE OF WALES, LORD JOHN OF LANCASTER,
*   * SIR WALTER BLUNT, *and* FALSTAFF

KING How bloodily the sun begins to peer
        Above yon bulky hill. The day looks pale
        At his distemperature.
PRINCE   The southern wind
        Doth play the trumpet to his purposes,
        And by his hollow whistling in the leaves   5
        Foretells a tempest and a blust'ring day.
KING Then with the losers let it sympathise,
        For nothing can seem foul to those that win.
                The trumpet sounds

          Enter WORCESTER [*and* VERNON]

        How now, my Lord of Worcester! 'Tis not well
        That you and I should meet upon such terms   10
        As now we meet. You have deceived our trust,
        And made us doff our easy robes of peace
        To crush our old limbs in ungentle steel.
        This is not well, my lord, this is not well.
        What say you to it? Will you again unknit   15
        The churlish knot of all-abhorrèd war,
        And move in that obedient orb again
        Where you did give a fair and natural light,
        And be no more an exhal'd meteor,
        A prodigy of fear, and a portent   20
        Of broachèd mischief to the unborn times?
WORCESTER Hear me, my liege.
        For mine own part I could be well content
        To entertain the lag end of my life
        With quiet hours. For I protest   25
        I have not sought the day of this dislike.

Worcester explains why his family now rebels: they supported Henry who swore he wanted only to reclaim his rights as Duke of Lancaster. But Henry broke his oath and seized the crown.

1 'Peace, chewet, peace!'

Falstaff breaks into the serious business of politics to joke at Worcester's expense. The actor playing Hal can choose whether his rebuke is angry or friendly and amused ('chewet' is a jackdaw, or chatterbox, or meat pie!). How do you think Prince Hal should speak to Falstaff?

2 'Forgot your oath' (in pairs)

Worcester, like Hotspur before him (Act 4 Scene 3, lines 54–105), recapitulates the rebels' grievances against King Henry. The Percy family supported Henry when he returned from exile to claim his inheritance on the death of his father, John of Gaunt. Henry swore a solemn oath at Doncaster that he wanted only what was his by right, the Dukedom of Lancaster. But he broke his solemn vow and took advantage of King Richard II's misfortunes to seize the crown.

An actor who played Worcester said 'I found in rehearsal that a major clue to this speech is to emphasise every 'you' and 'your', and 'we' and 'our' and to point at Henry or to myself at each of the pronouns.'

Take his advice, and emphasise each personal pronoun and add an appropriate gesture.

3 Cuckoo in the nest

The cuckoo lays an egg in the nest of a smaller bird. When the cuckoo's egg hatches, the chick pushes all the other eggs or chicks out of the nest, so that it gets all the food its foster parents bring. How does Henry react to Worcester's image in lines 59–64?

---

remember remind
posted galloped fast
in place and in account in status and regard
new-fallen right recent inheritance (by the death of his father)
wanton time chaotic time

seeming sufferances apparent wrongs
occasion opportunity
gripe the general sway seize total power
durst dared
head army

KING You have not sought it? How comes it, then?
FALSTAFF Rebellion lay in his way, and he found it.
PRINCE Peace, chewet, peace!
WORCESTER It pleased your majesty to turn your looks   30
　　　　　Of favour from myself, and all our house,
　　　　　And yet I must remember you, my lord,
　　　　　We were the first and dearest of your friends.
　　　　　For you my staff of office did I break
　　　　　In Richard's time, and posted day and night   35
　　　　　To meet you on the way, and kiss your hand,
　　　　　When yet you were in place and in account
　　　　　Nothing so strong and fortunate as I.
　　　　　It was myself, my brother, and his son,
　　　　　That brought you home, and boldly did outdare   40
　　　　　The dangers of the time. You swore to us,
　　　　　And you did swear that oath at Doncaster,
　　　　　That you did nothing purpose 'gainst the state,
　　　　　Nor claim no further than your new-fallen right,
　　　　　The seat of Gaunt, dukedom of Lancaster.   45
　　　　　To this we swore our aid. But in short space
　　　　　It rained down fortune showering on your head,
　　　　　And such a flood of greatness fell on you,
　　　　　What with our help, what with the absent King,
　　　　　What with the injuries of a wanton time,   50
　　　　　The seeming sufferances that you had borne,
　　　　　And the contrarious winds that held the King
　　　　　So long in his unlucky Irish wars
　　　　　That all in England did repute him dead.
　　　　　And from this swarm of fair advantages   55
　　　　　You took occasion to be quickly wooed
　　　　　To gripe the general sway into your hand,
　　　　　Forgot your oath to us at Doncaster,
　　　　　And being fed by us, you used us so
　　　　　As that ungentle gull the cuckoo's bird   60
　　　　　Useth the sparrow – did oppress our nest,
　　　　　Grew by our feeding to so great a bulk
　　　　　That even our love durst not come near your sight
　　　　　For fear of swallowing. But with nimble wing
　　　　　We were enforced for safety's sake to fly   65
　　　　　Out of your sight, and raise this present head,

King Henry replies that the rebellion has given many undesirable people pleasure at the prospect of chaos and looting. Hal praises Hotspur and offers to fight him in single combat to avoid greater bloodshed.

1 King Henry's reply (in pairs)

Henry rejects Worcester's long catalogue of grievances. He claims that they merely 'face the garment of rebellion': decorate the rebels' true intentions like fancy patches on a coat. They appeal to discontented rascals who are looking for opportunities to loot ('pell-mell havoc') in the chaos that will result.

Such ne'er-do-wells and 'fickle changelings' (turncoats, untrustworthy supporters) 'rub the elbow' at the prospect of violent rebellion ('hurly-burly innovation'). In Shakespeare's time, rubbing the elbows as if they itched was a sign of delight (today, people often rub their hands at the prospect of something pleasing).

Speak Henry's lines as forcefully and contemptuously as you can. Then talk together about whether Henry is answering Worcester's charges, or merely blustering to conceal his own wrongdoing. It can help your thinking to consider how far you agree with the following assessment:

> 'Lines 72–82 are a typical politician's speech. He doesn't address the point at issue, but veers off into blaming anyone except himself and using very emotive language to persuade by fear.'

2 The voice of chivalry?

Hal praises Hotspur and offers to meet him in single combat like the knights of medieval chivalry. Explore ways of speaking Hal's lines to find an appropriate style of delivery. Do you think his praise of Hotspur is sincere?

---

forged created
unkind unnatural
dangerous countenance hostile
  appearance
troth solemn promises
younger enterprise first intentions

articulate listed
This present ... head excluding
  blame for this rebellion
odds advantage
estimation reputation

Whereby we stand opposèd, by such means
As you yourself have forged against yourself,
By unkind usage, dangerous countenance,
And violation of all faith and troth   70
Sworn to us in your younger enterprise.

KING These things indeed you have articulate,
Proclaimed at market crosses, read in churches,
To face the garment of rebellion
With some fine colour that may please the eye   75
Of fickle changelings and poor discontents,
Which gape and rub the elbow at the news
Of hurly-burly innovation.
And never yet did insurrection want
Such water-colours to impaint his cause,   80
Nor moody beggars starving for a time
Of pell-mell havoc and confusion.

PRINCE In both your armies there is many a soul
Shall pay full dearly for this encounter
If once they join in trial. Tell your nephew,   85
The Prince of Wales doth join with all the world
In praise of Henry Percy. By my hopes,
This present enterprise set off his head,
I do not think a braver gentleman,
More active-valiant or more valiant-young,   90
More daring or more bold, is now alive
To grace this latter age with noble deeds.
For my part, I may speak it to my shame,
I have a truant been to chivalry,
And so I hear he doth account me too.   95
Yet this before my father's majesty –
I am content that he shall take the odds
Of his great name and estimation,
And will, to save the blood on either side,
Try fortune with him in a single fight.   100

King Henry offers friendship to the rebels if they lay down their arms.
Hal predicts the rebels will fight, and Henry orders preparation. Falstaff,
fearing the battle, reflects ironically on honour.

1 Good faith? Bad faith?

Is King Henry's offer of peace made sincerely or cynically? Experiment with two ways of delivering his speech. In the first he genuinely wants peace. In the second he has no intention of befriending the rebels. Do you prefer one interpretation over the other?

2 'Honour' (in small groups)

Falstaff's soliloquy (lines 127–38) exposes the emptiness of 'honour', and ironically contrasts with how Hotspur and Hal regard honour. Prepare a presentation of the lines thinking about whether Falstaff speaks directly to the audience, or to himself, or ...?

a Identify a chosen audience and speak the lines to that audience. For example: an anti-war rally, a reunion of war veterans, a television broadcast and so on.

b Speak aloud Hotspur's lines on honour in Act 1 Scene 3, lines 199–205 as a contrast to Falstaff's. Try intercutting the two speeches to make a single presentation in which one man's viewpoint comments ironically on the other's. The following can help your preparation:

'pricks me on' (line 129) – spurs me forward

'prick me off' (line 130) – mark me down for death (by piercing a hole through my name on a list)

'scutcheon' (line 138) – painted coat of arms displayed at a funeral

'catechism' (line 138) – question and answer technique (as used in teaching religion)

---

venture support
Rebuke and dread correction
  harsh punishment
Colossus a giant statue at the
  harbour of Rhodes whose legs
  bestrode the harbour entrance

forward ready to meet
set to mend
trim reckoning neat conclusion
  (spoken ironically)
Detraction slander

KING And, Prince of Wales, so dare we venture thee,
   Albeit considerations infinite
   Do make against it. No, good Worcester, no,
   We love our people well, even those we love
   That are misled upon your cousin's part,   105
   And will they take the offer of our grace,
   Both he, and they, and you, yea, every man
   Shall be my friend again, and I'll be his.
   So tell your cousin, and bring me word
   What he will do. But if he will not yield,   110
   Rebuke and dread correction wait on us,
   And they shall do their office. So, be gone.
   We will not now be troubled with reply.
   We offer fair, take it advisedly.
         Exeunt Worcester [and Vernon]

PRINCE It will not be accepted, on my life.   115
   The Douglas and the Hotspur both together
   Are confident against the world in arms.

KING Hence, therefore, every leader to his charge,
   For on their answer will we set on them,
   And God befriend us as our cause is just!   120
      Exeunt; the Prince and Falstaff remain

FALSTAFF Hal, if thou see me down in the battle and bestride me so,
 'tis a point of friendship.

PRINCE Nothing but a Colossus can do thee that friendship.
 Say thy prayers, and farewell.

FALSTAFF I would 'twere bed-time, Hal, and all well.   125

PRINCE Why, thou owest God a death.   *[Exit]*

FALSTAFF 'Tis not due yet – I would be loath to pay him before his
 day. What need I be so forward with him that calls not on me?
 Well, 'tis no matter, honour pricks me on. Yea, but how if honour
 prick me off when I come on, how then? Can honour set to a leg? 130
 No. Or an arm? No. Or take away the grief of a wound? No.
 Honour hath no skill in surgery then? No. What is honour? A
 word. What is in that word honour? What is that honour? Air. A
 trim reckoning! Who hath it? He that died a' Wednesday. Doth he
 feel it? No. Doth he hear it? No. 'Tis insensible, then? Yea, to the 135
 dead. But will it not live with the living? No. Why? Detraction
 will not suffer it. Therefore I'll none of it. Honour is a mere
 scutcheon – and so ends my catechism.   *Exit*

...decides not to tell Hotspur of King Henry's peace offer because ...gh Hotspur may be excused, Worcester and Northumberland will be always suspected and finally executed.

1 Honour? (in pairs)

Falstaff ended the previous scene saying 'Honour is a mere scutcheon'. Now Worcester's deceit confirms the view that honour is no more than a painted board at a funeral, merely a show. For his own self-protection, Worcester decides not to tell Hotspur that King Henry is ready to make peace and pardon all the rebels.

Worcester has to persuade Vernon to agree to his plan to deceive Hotspur. Step into his role in turn and speak his lines 3–25 as convincingly as you can.

2 Worcester's imagery

Worcester's speech is rich in imagery. He uses striking metaphors and similes (see page 197). Match the following with appropriate lines:

- we will always be under surveillance
- we will be regarded like a fox, whose instinct can never be trusted
- our outward appearances will be wrongly 'read'
- like cattle, the better we are treated, the nearer we are to slaughter
- Hotspur is unpredictable
- we are the source of all Hotspur's offences.

3 Assessing character (in small groups)

a Would you trust King Henry's word? Give reasons for your reply.

b 'This speech shows Worcester as he really is: a cold, calculating politician.' How far do you agree?

c Why does Vernon agree (line 26)? Is he 'honourable?'

---

still always
Supposition suspicious people
wild trick inherited savagery
misquote wrongly read
My nephew's trespass Hotspur's offence

an adopted name of privilege a nickname that protects him
spleen rash temper
ta'en caught
spring of all source of corruption

ACT 5   SCENE 2
Shrewsbury: the rebels' camp

Enter WORCESTER, *and* SIR RICHARD VERNON

WORCESTER O no, my nephew must not know, Sir Richard,
    The liberal and kind offer of the King.
VERNON 'Twere best he did.
WORCESTER   Then are we all undone.
    It is not possible, it cannot be,
    The King should keep his word in loving us.   5
    He will suspect us still, and find a time
    To punish this offence in other faults.
    Supposition all our lives shall be stuck full of eyes,
    For treason is but trusted like the fox,
    Who, never so tame, so cherished and locked up,   10
    Will have a wild trick of his ancestors.
    Look how we can, or sad or merrily,
    Interpretation will misquote our looks,
    And we shall feed like oxen at a stall,
    The better cherished still the nearer death.   15
    My nephew's trespass may be well forgot,
    It hath the excuse of youth and heat of blood,
    And an adopted name of privilege –
    A hare-brained Hotspur, governed by a spleen.
    All his offences live upon my head   20
    And on his father's. We did train him on,
    And, his corruption being ta'en from us,
    We as the spring of all shall pay for all.
    Therefore, good cousin, let not Harry know
    In any case the offer of the King.   25
              Enter HOTSPUR *and* DOUGLAS
VERNON Deliver what you will; I'll say 'tis so.
    Here comes your cousin.
HOTSPUR   My uncle is returned;
    Deliver up my Lord of Westmoreland.
    Uncle, what news?

Worcester lies about King Henry's reply and tells of Hal's challenge to single combat. Vernon praises Hal for his generous descriptions of Hotspur, his self-criticism and his promise as a future king.

1 Truth and lies (in pairs)

Worcester speaks nine lines opposite. How many contain lies, how many contain truth? (In line 38, 'forswearing that he is forsworn' means 'denying he broke his promises'.)

2 'A brave defiance'

Westmoreland has been held as hostage ('engaged') to ensure Worcester's safe return from the king's camp. Douglas tells Westmoreland to carry Hotspur's message of defiance to the king. Write the speech that Douglas spoke to Westmoreland. Use lines 41–4 as your inspiration.

3 Sir Richard Vernon

Vernon again describes Prince Hal in glowing terms. He recounts Hal's praise of Hotspur, which Hal acknowledged could never match Hotspur himself ('dispraising praise valued with you'). And he relates how Hal made a 'blushing cital' (shame-faced criticism) of himself with impressive grace.

Compare Vernon's speech opposite with his earlier praise of Hal in Act 4 Scene 1, lines 97–110. Then turn the page to find how Hotspur responds, and suggest two or three reasons of your own why Shakespeare gives such a flattering speech to Vernon. Think about Vernon's character, his dramatic function, and what his lines suggest about Hal.

---

presently immediately
seeming mercy appearance of
 forgiveness
haughty arms noble soldiers
Harry Monmouth (Prince Hal
 was born at Monmouth)
tasking challenge

proof of arms combat
Trimmed up sang
chronicle history book
chid rebuked
envy malice
misconstrued wrongly understood

WORCESTER The King will bid you battle presently.   30
DOUGLAS Defy him by the Lord of Westmoreland.
HOTSPUR Lord Douglas, go you and tell him so.
DOUGLAS Marry, and shall, and very willingly.   *Exit*
WORCESTER There is no seeming mercy in the King.
HOTSPUR Did you beg any? God forbid!   35
WORCESTER I told him gently of our grievances,
   Of his oath-breaking – which he mended thus,
   By now forswearing that he is forsworn.
   He calls us rebels, traitors, and will scourge
   With haughty arms this hateful name in us.   40

    Enter DOUGLAS

DOUGLAS Arm, gentlemen, to arms! For I have thrown
   A brave defiance in King Henry's teeth,
   And Westmoreland that was engaged did bear it,
   Which cannot choose but bring him quickly on.
WORCESTER The Prince of Wales stepped forth before the King,   45
   And, nephew, challenged you to single fight.
HOTSPUR O, would the quarrel lay upon our heads,
   And that no man might draw short breath today
   But I and Harry Monmouth! Tell me, tell me,
   How showed his tasking? Seemed it in contempt?   50
VERNON No, by my soul, I never in my life
   Did hear a challenge urged more modestly,
   Unless a brother should a brother dare
   To gentle exercise and proof of arms.
   He gave you all the duties of a man,   55
   Trimmed up your praises with a princely tongue,
   Spoke your deservings like a chronicle,
   Making you ever better than his praise
   By still dispraising praise valued with you,
   And, which became him like a prince indeed,   60
   He made a blushing cital of himself,
   And chid his truant youth with such a grace
   As if he mastered there a double spirit
   Of teaching and of learning instantly.
   There did he pause. But let me tell the world –   65
   If he outlive the envy of this day,
   England did never owe so sweet a hope
   So much misconstrued in his wantonness.

Hotspur dismisses Vernon's praise of Hal, and predicts he will kill the Prince. He urges his troops to battle assuring them their cause is just, even though death threatens.

1 Hotspur the warrior

Here's how an actor who played Hotspur described his approach to speaking Hotspur's lines. Use his comments to work out your own preferred style of delivery.

'Hotspur shows that he isn't just a simple soldier, but that he has political skill. He runs through a range of styles and tones:
– contemptuous dismissal followed by menacing irony (lines 69–74)
– urgency ('Arm, arm with speed!')
– self-criticism that everyone knows is not sincere but humorous (lines 75–8)
– inspiring motivation followed by reassuring sincerity (lines 81–8)
– more humorous self-criticism (lines 90–1)
– ever-increasing rallying call to battle (lines 92–100)'

2 True or false?

Hotspur claims he is no orator, saying he has 'not well the gift of tongue' to inspire his soldiers by persuasion (lines 76–8), and 'I profess not talking' (line 91). Do you believe him? Give your own impression of Hotspur's skill with words, using actual examples of his language.

3 Building up tension (in pairs)

Shakespeare's language builds up the sense of a rapidly approaching battle, as do his stage directions. Identify on the opposite page some of the ways in which a growing sense of urgency is created. Suggest some stage business that could accompany Hotspur's lines to create the feeling of growing tension at the prospect of imminent combat.

---

enamoured/On his follies! in love with his faults
liberty libertine, reprobate, degenerate
basely dishonourably
dial's point clock hand

intent of bearing them reason for fighting
temper fine steel
Esperance! Hope! (the war cry of the Percy family)
heaven to earth as sure as heaven is different from earth

HOTSPUR Cousin, I think thou art enamoured
        On his follies! Never did I hear   70
        Of any prince so wild a liberty.
        But be he as he will, yet once ere night
        I will embrace him with a soldier's arm,
        That he shall shrink under my courtesy.
        Arm, arm with speed! And fellows, soldiers, friends,   75
        Better consider what you have to do
        Than I that have not well the gift of tongue
        Can lift your blood up with persuasion.

Enter a MESSENGER

[FIRST] MESSENGER My lord, here are letters for you.
HOTSPUR I cannot read them now.   80
        O gentlemen, the time of life is short!
        To spend that shortness basely were too long
        If life did ride upon a dial's point,
        Still ending at the arrival of an hour.
        And if we live, we live to tread on kings,   85
        If die, brave death when princes die with us!
        Now, for our consciences, the arms are fair
        When the intent of bearing them is just.

Enter another [MESSENGER]

[SECOND] MESSENGER My lord, prepare, the King comes on apace.
HOTSPUR I thank him that he cuts me from my tale,   90
        For I profess not talking. Only this –
        Let each man do his best. And here draw I
        A sword whose temper I intend to stain
        With the best blood that I can meet withal
        In the adventure of this perilous day.   95
        Now, Esperance! Percy! and set on!
        Sound all the lofty instruments of war,
        And by that music let us all embrace,
        For, heaven to earth, some of us never shall
        A second time do such a courtesy.   100
        Here they embrace, the trumpets sound
                            [Exeunt]

Douglas kills Sir Walter Blunt, who is disguised as King Henry.
Hotspur praises Douglas, but reveals that there are many knights in
disguise as Henry. Douglas vows to kill them all.

1 Staging the battle (in small groups)

In the theatre, the action of battle flows rapidly from the end of
Scene 2 into Scenes 3 and 4. Every production faces the problem of
how to present the constantly changing events of the combat. Amid all
the comings and goings, raids and attacks, are a number of distinct
sequences.

In Scene 3, there are five episodes: the fight of Douglas and Blunt,
Hotspur and Douglas' conversation, Falstaff's soliloquy, the encounter
of Hal and Falstaff, and Falstaff's exit soliloquy. Work out how to stage
the scene so that the action flows effectively. It may be best to rehearse
each short episode separately, then work out how they can fit together
on stage. As you prepare think about the following:

- how Shakespeare dramatises comic and serious episodes in the
  battle.
- how the concept of 'honour' applies to each episode.
- how you would wish the audience to respond to line 27.
- how you will get the dead bodies off the stage.

2 Decoys and counterfeits

King Henry has many of his troops disguised as himself on the
battlefield. Say why you think Henry has ordered this deception, and
what it suggests about the nature of the battle and Henry's character.

Alarum call to battle by drums
  and trumpets
dear ... hath ... likeness
  died for resembling the king
a yielder someone who surrenders

Semblably furnished
  similar in armour and weapons
borrowed title false kingship
coats surcoats, sleeveless tunics
  worn over armour

ACT 5 SCENE 3
Shrewsbury: the battlefield

The KING *enters with his power. Alarum to the battle. Then enter* DOUGLAS *and* SIR WALTER BLUNT *[disguised as the king]*

BLUNT What is thy name that in the battle thus
        Thou crossest me? What honour dost thou seek
        Upon my head?
DOUGLAS   Know then my name is Douglas,
        And I do haunt thee in the battle thus
        Because some tell me that thou art a king.   5
BLUNT They tell thee true.
DOUGLAS The Lord of Stafford dear today hath bought
        Thy likeness, for instead of thee, King Harry,
        This sword hath ended him: so shall it thee
        Unless thou yield thee as my prisoner.   10
BLUNT I was not born a yielder, thou proud Scot,
        And thou shalt find a king that will revenge
        Lord Stafford's death.
              They fight; Douglas kills Blunt

           Then enter HOTSPUR

HOTSPUR O Douglas, hadst thou fought at Holmedon thus
        I never had triumphed upon a Scot.   15
DOUGLAS All's done, all's won. Here breathless lies the King.
HOTSPUR Where?
DOUGLAS Here.
HOTSPUR This, Douglas? No, I know this face full well.
        A gallant knight he was, his name was Blunt,   20
        Semblably furnished like the King himself.
DOUGLAS A fool go with thy soul, whither it goes!
        A borrowed title hast thou bought too dear.
        Why didst thou tell me that thou wert a king?
HOTSPUR The King hath many marching in his coats.   25
DOUGLAS Now, by my sword, I will kill all his coats!
        I'll murder all his wardrobe, piece by piece,
        Until I meet the King.

The sight of the dead Sir Walter Blunt prompts Falstaff to reflect ironically on honour and to fear for his life. Hal is not amused by Falstaff's joking. Falstaff broods on the future.

1 'God keep lead out of me' (in small groups)

Typically, Falstaff begins with two puns. In London, he could get away without paying his tavern bill (the 'shot' or 'score'). In the battle he also hopes to escape 'shot-free', but now the 'shot' are very real flying bullets, all too likely to 'score' a hit on him.

a Almost all Falstaff's soldiers have been killed. The few remaining soldiers will become beggars around the outskirts of their towns. What do you think Falstaff actually did when he claims to have 'led' his ragged soldiers into the killing fields at Shrewsbury?

b Speak both of Falstaff's soliloquies to discover an appropriate style for each. Think about how much you would want to make an audience laugh, and how much you would want them to be affected by the anti-war tone of Falstaff's words.

2 A joke too far? (in small groups)

Describe your reaction to Hal's line 52 ('What, is it a time to jest and dally now?'). Do you feel more sympathy for Hal or Falstaff at this moment?

3 'Turk Gregory'

None can be sure who Falstaff has in mind when he compares himself to 'Turk Gregory' (lines 43–4). 'Turk' was often used by Elizabethans to describe any violent or cruel man. Gregory might be a Pope: either Gregory VII (1073) who had a furious temper, or Gregory XIII who died in 1585 and had promised forgiveness to anyone who assassinated Queen Elizabeth.

---

pate head
Here's no vanity! This is for real!
peppered shot to pieces
vaunting proud, boastful
paid killed

sack (line 51) destroy
pierce (pronounced 'perce')
make a carbonado of me
  slice me up

HOTSPUR   Up and away!
　　　Our soldiers stand full fairly for the day.

　　　　　　　　　　　　　　　　　　　　　　[Exeunt]
　　　　　　　Alarum. Enter FALSTAFF *alone*

FALSTAFF Though I could scape shot-free at London, I fear the shot   30
　　here, here's no scoring but upon the pate. Soft! Who are you? Sir
　　Walter Blunt – there's honour for you! Here's no vanity! I am as
　　hot as molten lead, and as heavy too. God keep lead out of me, I
　　need no more weight than mine own bowels. I have led my
　　ragamuffins where they are peppered. There's not three of my   35
　　hundred-and-fifty left alive – and they are for the town's end, to
　　beg during life. But who comes here?

　　　　　　　　　　　Enter the PRINCE

PRINCE What, stand'st thou idle here? Lend me thy sword.
　　Many a nobleman lies stark and stiff
　　Under the hoofs of vaunting enemies,   40
　　Whose deaths are yet unrevenged. I prithee
　　Lend me thy sword.
FALSTAFF O Hal, I prithee give me leave to breathe a while. Turk
　　Gregory never did such deeds in arms as I have done this day. I
　　have paid Percy, I have made him sure.   45
PRINCE He is indeed, and living to kill thee.
　　I prithee lend me thy sword.
FALSTAFF Nay, before God, Hal, if Percy be alive thou gets not my
　　sword, but take my pistol if thou wilt.
PRINCE Give it me. What, is it in the case?   50
FALSTAFF Aye, Hal, 'tis hot, 'tis hot. There's that will sack a city.
　　　　The Prince draws it out, and finds it to be a bottle of sack
PRINCE What, is it a time to jest and dally now?
　　　　　　　He throws the bottle at him   *Exit*
FALSTAFF Well, if Percy be alive, I'll pierce him. If he do come in my
　　way, so. If he do not, if I come in his willingly, let him make a
　　carbonado of me. I like not such grinning honour as Sir Walter   55
　　hath. Give me life, which if I can save, so. If not, honour comes
　　unlooked for, and there's an end.
　　　　　　　　　　　　　　　　　　　　　　[Exit]

Hal, wounded, refuses to return to his tent, and praises the bravery of his brother John. Douglas challenges King Henry, determined to kill him.

---

1 'Alarum. Excursions' (in small groups)

The action of the scene flows swiftly from the end of the previous scene. 'Alarums' are trumpet calls to battle, and 'Excursions' are flurries of fighting between groups of soldiers.

Hal has been wounded in one of these encounters. Decide whether you would show the incident in which he was wounded, and just how serious a wound he receives. Work out how to stage the sequence, and state what impression you hope your staging would create on the audience.

2 Prince John

Lord John of Lancaster is Hal's younger brother. At the time of the historical battle of Shrewsbury (1403) he was only thirteen years old and took no part in the conflict.

Earlier in the play (Act 3 Scene 2, lines 32–3) King Henry says that John had taken Hal's place on the king's Council, because Hal had been dismissed for his riotous behaviour. John plays a large part in *Henry IV Part 2*, and also appears (as the Duke of Bedford) in *Henry V*, where he fights at Agincourt. He is also in *Henry VI Part 1* as the Regent (ruler) of France.

Historically, John is probably best known for playing a major part in the capture and execution of Joan of Arc. But Shakespeare transfers those actions to the Duke of York in *Henry VI Part 1*, and shows Joan mocking the sick and old Bedford as 'good grey beard'.

Speak everything John (Lancaster) says and what is said about him in lines 1–23. Suggest what kind of character you think Shakespeare is trying to create.

---

make up advance
retirement retreat
amaze dismay, alarm
stained nobility wounded
 warriors, dishonoured noblemen
breathe rest
the point sword's end

lustier maintenance more
 vigorous effort
mettle courage, spirit
Hydra (in Greek mythology) a
 many-headed monster. When one
 head was cut off, it grew two others
those colours the king's emblems

ACT 5 SCENE 4
Shrewsbury: the battlefield

Alarum. Excursions. Enter the KING, *the* PRINCE, LORD JOHN OF
LANCASTER, *and* EARL OF WESTMORELAND

KING I prithee, Harry, withdraw thyself, thou bleedest too much.
    Lord John of Lancaster, go you with him.
LANCASTER Not I, my lord, unless I did bleed too.
PRINCE I beseech your majesty, make up,
    Lest your retirement do amaze your friends.   5
KING I will do so. My Lord of Westmoreland,
    Lead him to his tent.
WESTMORELAND Come, my lord, I'll lead you to your tent.
PRINCE Lead me, my lord? I do not need your help,
    And God forbid a shallow scratch should drive   10
    The Prince of Wales from such a field as this,
    Where stained nobility lies trodden on,
    And rebels' arms triumph in massacres!
LANCASTER We breathe too long: come, cousin Westmoreland,
    Our duty this way lies: for God's sake, come.   15
           [Exeunt Lancaster and Westmoreland]
PRINCE By God, thou hast deceived me, Lancaster,
    I did not think thee lord of such a spirit:
    Before, I loved thee as a brother, John,
    But now I do respect thee as my soul.
KING I saw him hold Lord Percy at the point   20
    With lustier maintenance than I did look for
    Of such an ungrown warrior.
PRINCE O, this boy lends mettle to us all!   *Exit*

[Enter DOUGLAS*]*

DOUGLAS Another king! They grow like Hydra's heads.
    I am the Douglas, fatal to all those   25
    That wear those colours on them. What art thou
    That counterfeitest the person of a king?

King Henry defies Douglas, but is in danger of being killed by him. Hal intervenes and saves the king's life. Henry acknowledges that Hal loves him and has won back his lost honour.

1 Saving the king (in small groups)

Work out how to stage the fight in which Douglas almost kills King Henry. Hal should arrive just in the nick of time to rescue his father and reveal something of the character of Douglas. What sort of fight does Douglas put up with Hal? Remember that safety is the prime consideration in all stage fighting. Many productions stage the fight in slow motion, freezing the action at particular points to make striking tableaux.

2 Who's who?

Of the five noblemen named opposite, only Blunt appears in the play. He was killed by Douglas in the previous scene. Shirley and Stafford were also decoys dressed as the king, killed by Douglas.

Sir Nicholas Gawsey and Clifton are noblemen fighting on the king's side. Both were reported by Holinshed to be killed at Shrewsbury (see page 200).

Imagine the actor playing Hal says to you 'I don't see how the lines about Clifton and Sir Nicholas Gawsey add anything to the scene. Can we cut them in performance?' Make your reply.

3 Murder in mind?

Lines 50–6 may seem puzzling, because there is no incident in the play where someone says that Hal wished King Henry was dead. Historically, there was a rumour that Hal tried to kill his father. From what you know of Hal, does the rumour seem likely to be true?

---

shadows decoys, imitations (now dead)
assay test
fares goes
succour help

opinion reputation
mak'st some tender of care for
hearkened for desired
Make up go

KING The King himself, who, Douglas, grieves at heart
        So many of his shadows thou hast met,
        And not the very King. I have two boys   30
        Seek Percy and thyself about the field,
        But seeing thou fallest on me so luckily
        I will assay thee, and defend thyself.
DOUGLAS I fear thou art another counterfeit,
        And yet, in faith, thou bearest thee like a king –   35
        But mine I am sure thou art, whoe'er thou be,
        And thus I win thee.
                They fight, the King being in danger

                Enter PRINCE OF WALES

PRINCE Hold up thy head, vile Scot, or thou art like
        Never to hold it up again! The spirits
        Of valiant Shirley, Stafford, Blunt are in my arms.   40
        It is the Prince of Wales that threatens thee,
        Who never promiseth but he means to pay.
                They fight; Douglas flieth
        Cheerly, my lord, how fares your grace?
        Sir Nicholas Gawsey hath for succour sent,
        And so hath Clifton – I'll to Clifton straight.   45
KING Stay and breathe a while.
        Thou hast redeemed thy lost opinion,
        And showed thou mak'st some tender of my life
        In this fair rescue thou hast brought to me.
PRINCE O God, they did me too much injury   50
        That ever said I hearkened for your death.
        If it were so, I might have let alone
        The insulting hand of Douglas over you,
        Which would have been as speedy in your end
        As all the poisonous potions in the world,   55
        And saved the treacherous labour of your son.
KING Make up to Clifton, I'll to Sir Nicholas Gawsey.
                                                        Exit

Hotspur regrets that Hal has fewer honours than himself. Douglas fights Falstaff and appears to kill him. Hotspur, mortally wounded, regrets the loss of his honours more than the loss of his life.

1 Harry to Harry (in pairs)

In Act 4 Scene 1, lines 122–3, Hotspur had longed for the moment in which he would confront Hal:

> Harry to Harry shall, hot horse to horse,
> Meet and ne'er part till one drop down a corpse.

Now Hotspur and Hal finally come face to face, their first and only meeting. After an exchange of chivalrous bragging, they fight each other. Work out how to stage lines 58–76 to show how Hotspur and Hal speak to each other and how they fight.

2 A comic parallel (in pairs)

In the fight of Douglas and Falstaff, Shakespeare provides a comic parallel to the combat of Hal and Hotspur. Every production spends much time rehearsing how the two fights are staged. Actors and directors plan the effect they hope to have on the audience through the combination of the serious and comic plots.

Just how would you present the fight between Douglas and Falstaff?

3 Hotspur's dying words

Explore different ways of speaking Hotspur's death speech. The actor Laurence Olivier played Hotspur as a man who had difficulty pronouncing the letter 'w'. Try speaking Hotspur's lines in the same fashion, remembering that the final word he wishes to speak is 'worms'.

---

one sphere the same orbit
brook tolerate
budding honours on thy crest favours, signs of nobility on your helmet

crop cut
brittle frail, human
takes survey of sees, dominates, commands

Enter HOTSPUR

HOTSPUR If I mistake not, thou art Harry Monmouth.
PRINCE Thou speakest as if I would deny my name.
HOTSPUR My name is Harry Percy.
PRINCE   Why then I see   60
    A very valiant rebel of the name.
    I am the Prince of Wales, and think not, Percy,
    To share with me in glory any more.
    Two stars keep not their motion in one sphere,
    Nor can one England brook a double reign   65
    Of Harry Percy and the Prince of Wales.
HOTSPUR Nor shall it, Harry, for the hour is come
    To end the one of us; and would to God
    Thy name in arms were now as great as mine.
PRINCE I'll make it greater ere I part from thee,   70
    And all the budding honours on thy crest
    I'll crop to make a garland for my head.
HOTSPUR I can no longer brook thy vanities.
               They fight

Enter FALSTAFF

FALSTAFF Well said, Hal! To it, Hal! Nay, you shall find no
    boy's play here, I can tell you.   75

Enter DOUGLAS; *he fighteth with* FALSTAFF, [*who*] *falls
down as if he were dead*

                             [*Exit Douglas*]
            The Prince killeth Percy
HOTSPUR O Harry, thou hast robbed me of my youth!
    I better brook the loss of brittle life
    Than those proud titles thou hast won of me.
    They wound my thoughts worse than thy sword my flesh.
    But thoughts, the slaves of life, and life, time's fool,   80
    And time, that takes survey of all the world,
    Must have a stop. O, I could prophesy,
    But that the earthy and cold hand of death
    Lies on my tongue. No, Percy, thou art dust,
    And food for –   85
              [*He dies*]

Hal praises the dead Hotspur as braver than any man who lives. In tribute, he places his helmet plumes on Hotspur's face. His farewell to Falstaff puns on Falstaff's size.

Hal's farewell to Hotspur uses language suitable to a noble opponent. He lays his 'favours' (the plumes or ribbons from his helmet) on Hotspur's face as a mark of respect. His farewell to Falstaff reflects his relationship with the fat knight, expressing humour as much as sorrow.

Ill-weaved ... shrunk (badly woven cloth shrinks when washed)
bound limit
stout brave
sensible of courtesy alive to hear my compliments
zeal praise

fair rites kind ceremonies
ignominy shame
epitaph memorial on a tombstone
vanity frivolity
Embowelled disembowelled for embalming

PRINCE   For worms, brave Percy. Fare thee well, great heart!
          Ill-weaved ambition, how much art thou shrunk.
          When that this body did contain a spirit,
          A kingdom for it was too small a bound.
          But now two paces of the vilest earth   90
          Is room enough. This earth that bears thee dead
          Bears not alive so stout a gentleman.
          If thou wert sensible of courtesy
          I should not make so dear a show of zeal,
          But let my favours hide thy mangled face,   95
          And even in thy behalf I'll thank myself
          For doing these fair rites of tenderness.
          Adieu, and take thy praise with thee to heaven!
          Thy ignominy sleep with thee in the grave,
          But not remembered in thy epitaph.   100
               He spieth Falstaff on the ground
          What, old acquaintance, could not all this flesh
          Keep in a little life? Poor Jack, farewell!
          I could have better spared a better man.
          O, I should have a heavy miss of thee
          If I were much in love with vanity.   105
          Death hath not struck so fat a deer today,
          Though many dearer, in this bloody fray.
          Embowelled will I see thee by and by,
          Till then in blood by noble Percy lie.   *Exit*

Falstaff explains why he pretended to be dead: common sense overruled bravery. What seemed cowardice was wise caution. He stabs the dead Hotspur and claims to have killed him. Hal denies Falstaff's claim.

1 Dead or alive?

'Embowelled?' is always a great moment of theatre. In any audience there will be people who do not know the play, and may think that Douglas really has killed Falstaff. And those who know the play watch eagerly for just how Falstaff rises from the dead.

Step into role as Falstaff, lie down, and explore ways of how you come to life and speak your first word 'Embowelled?'.

2 Stabbing Hotspur

Falstaff, about to stab the dead Hotspur says 'nobody sees me'. But he is being watched by every member of the audience! Many of them are shocked when Falstaff stabs the dead Hotspur. They find the action is cowardly and despicable. What is your reaction?

3 'There is Percy!'

Falstaff has carried Hotspur (Percy) off the battlefield in order to claim he killed him, and so be honoured by the king. The stage direction says that Falstaff 'lays' the body on the ground. But many editors change 'lays' to 'throws'. What would you do with Hotspur's body if you were playing Falstaff? Why?

4 'The better part of valour is discretion'

Line 117 has become a well-known proverb. What seems to be cowardice is really wise caution, and what seems be valour is foolish rashness. Try to think of an example from your own experience where you have acted with common sense and caution rather than with bravery.

---

powder pickle, salt
termagant violent and roaring
scot and lot totally
confutes me proves me wrong
fleshed initiated, made bloody

maiden never before used
double-man ghost
Jack villain
do me any honour reward me

Falstaff riseth up

FALSTAFF Embowelled? If thou embowel me today, I'll give you leave   110
to powder me and eat me too tomorrow. 'Sblood, 'twas time to
counterfeit, or that hot termagant Scot had paid me, scot and lot
too. Counterfeit? I lie, I am no counterfeit. To die is to be a
counterfeit, for he is but the counterfeit of a man who hath not the
life of a man. But to counterfeit dying, when a man thereby liveth,   115
is to be no counterfeit, but the true and perfect image of life
indeed. The better part of valour is discretion, in the which better
part I have saved my life. Zounds, I am afraid of this gunpowder
Percy, though he be dead. How if he should counterfeit too and
rise? By my faith, I am afraid he would prove the better counterfeit.   120
Therefore I'll make him sure, yea, and I'll swear I killed him. Why
may not he rise as well as I? Nothing confutes me but eyes, and
nobody sees me. Therefore, sirrah [*Stabbing him*], with a new
wound in your thigh, come you along with me.

He takes up Hotspur on his back

Enter PRINCE [*and*] JOHN OF LANCASTER

PRINCE Come, brother John, full bravely hast thou fleshed   125
    Thy maiden sword.
LANCASTER   But soft, whom have we here?
    Did you not tell me this fat man was dead?
PRINCE I did, I saw him dead,
    Breathless and bleeding on the ground. Art thou alive?
    Or is it fantasy that plays upon our eyesight?   130
    I prithee speak, we will not trust our eyes
    Without our ears. Thou art not what thou seemest.
FALSTAFF No, that's certain, I am not a double-man. But if I be not
Jack Falstaff, then am I a Jack. There is Percy!
    [*He lays the body on the ground*]
    If your father will do me any honour, so. If not, let him kill the next   135
Percy himself. I look to be either earl or duke, I can assure you.
PRINCE Why, Percy I killed myself, and saw thee dead.

Falstaff, in mock indignation, claims he fought Hotspur for an hour,
then killed him. Hal agrees to confirm the lie. Falstaff hopes for reward.
King Henry condemns Worcester's deceit.

1 Supporting a lie (in small groups)

Hal says that if Falstaff's claim that he killed Hotspur will gain him credit ('do thee grace'), he, the Prince, will confirm it in glowing detail. But why does Hal decide to support Falstaff's lie, and just how does he speak lines 148–9?

Speak the two lines as an aside to Falstaff, then as a remark that John (and anyone else on stage) could hear. What do the different styles of delivery suggest about Hal's character, and about his relationship with Falstaff?

Also think about how Prince John (Lancaster) reacts. In one production he obviously believed Falstaff, and so treated Hal with contempt, thinking his brother had lied about killing Hotspur.

2 'I'll purge'

Falstaff's intention (line 154) may be to repent for his sins, or to take medicine to become healthy. Do you think he will do either?

3 The final scene (in large groups)

Take parts and stage Scene 5 using the activities below and on page 182.

a Do the king and the others enter with dignity and ceremony, or are they exhausted and battle-stained?

b How are the captive Worcester and Vernon treated?

c Does King Henry deliver his criticism of Worcester standing or sitting, at a distance or close up, face to face?

---

your luggage the dead Hotspur
gild cover up, decorate
happiest terms most helpful words
retreat trumpet-call signalling end
  of battle
highest of the field highest ground

purge repent, take medicine
rebuke punishment
turn our offers contrary report
  the opposite
tenor spirit, nature
intelligence information

FALSTAFF Didst thou? Lord, Lord, how this world is given to lying! I
grant you I was down, and out of breath, and so was he, but we rose
both at an instant, and fought a long hour by Shrewsbury clock. If   140
I may be believed, so. If not, let them that should reward valour
bear the sin upon their own heads. I'll take it upon my death, I gave
him this wound in the thigh. If the man were alive, and would
deny it, zounds, I would make him eat a piece of my sword.
LANCASTER This is the strangest tale that ever I heard.   145
PRINCE This is the strangest fellow, brother John.
    Come, bring your luggage nobly on your back.
    For my part, if a lie may do thee grace,
    I'll gild it with the happiest terms I have.
               A retreat is sounded
    The trumpet sounds retreat, the day is ours.   150
    Come, brother, let us to the highest of the field,
    To see what friends are living, who are dead.
          Exeunt [Prince of Wales and Lancaster]
FALSTAFF I'll follow, as they say, for reward. He that rewards me, God
reward him! If I do grow great, I'll grow less, for I'll purge, and
leave sack, and live cleanly as a nobleman should do.   155
          Exit [bearing off the body]

ACT 5 SCENE 5
Shrewsbury: King Henry's camp

The trumpets sound. Enter the KING, PRINCE OF WALES,
LORD JOHN OF LANCASTER, EARL OF WESTMORELAND,
with WORCESTER *and* VERNON (*prisoners*)

KING Thus ever did rebellion find rebuke.
    Ill-spirited Worcester, did not we send grace,
    Pardon, and terms of love to all of you?
    And wouldst thou turn our offers contrary?
    Misuse the tenor of thy kinsman's trust?   5
    Three knights upon our party slain today,
    A noble earl, and many a creature else
    Had been alive this hour
    If like a Christian thou hadst truly borne
    Betwixt our armies true intelligence.   10

King Henry sentences Worcester and Vernon to death. Hal orders that the captured Douglas be set free to reward his bravery. The king prepares to fight the remaining rebels.

1 Is justice done? (in pairs)

Do Worcester, Vernon and Douglas deserve the 'justice' they receive? State what do you think about the treatment of each man, and suggest how they go to execution (proud and defiant, or ...?). How does King Henry react to Hal's pardoning of Douglas?

2 A final image (in groups of any size)

The final stage direction means 'everyone leaves the stage'. In one production Falstaff returned to rub his hands gleefully as he looked towards the departing Hal. In another production the sounds of the executioner's axe was heard as the sentence on Worcester and Vernon was carried out. A third production closed with a spotlight focused on three wounded soldiers, who had been on stage throughout the scene.

Think about the emotions you would wish an audience to feel as your own production of the play ends. Work out how each character leaves, and the final stage image that the audience sees.

3 Rebellion

Henry says 'Rebellion in this land shall lose his sway'. But Henry himself had rebelled against the rightful king, Richard II, and seized the throne. Imagine that the memory of his own rebellion comes into Henry's mind as he speaks line 41. How does he behave?

4 Unfinished business

The king's final speech looks forward to *Henry IV Part 2* which will show the effects of another rebellion. Turn to the map on page 2. Use it to prepare a battle plan based on Henry's lines 34–40.

---

pause upon delay judgement on
Upon the foot of fear running away in panic
honourable bounty honour of freeing Douglas
shown upon our crests evident in our wounds

in the bosom of when performed by
divide our power split up our army
prelate Scroop Archbishop of York
sway power
check defeat

WORCESTER What I have done my safety urged me to,
    And I embrace this fortune patiently,
    Since not to be avoided it falls on me.
KING Bear Worcester to the death, and Vernon too.
    Other offenders we will pause upon.   15

[Exeunt Worcester and Vernon guarded]

    How goes the field?
PRINCE The noble Scot, Lord Douglas, when he saw
    The fortune of the day quite turned from him,
    The noble Percy slain, and all his men
    Upon the foot of fear, fled with the rest,   20
    And falling from a hill he was so bruised
    That the pursuers took him. At my tent
    The Douglas is – and I beseech your grace
    I may dispose of him.
KING   With all my heart.
PRINCE Then, brother John of Lancaster, to you   25
    This honourable bounty shall belong.
    Go to the Douglas and deliver him
    Up to his pleasure, ransomless and free.
    His valours shown upon our crests today
    Have taught us how to cherish such high deeds,   30
    Even in the bosom of our adversaries.
LANCASTER I thank your grace for this high courtesy,
    Which I shall give away immediately.
KING Then this remains, that we divide our power.
    You, son John, and my cousin Westmoreland,   35
    Towards York shall bend you with your dearest speed
    To meet Northumberland and the prelate Scroop,
    Who, as we hear, are busily in arms.
    Myself and you, son Harry, will towards Wales,
    To fight with Glendower and the Earl of March.   40
    Rebellion in this land shall lose his sway,
    Meeting the check of such another day,
    And since this business so fair is done,
    Let us not leave till all our own be won.
                                  Exeunt

Looking back at the play
Activities for groups or individuals

1 Change the title

All Shakespeare's history plays are titled by the name of a king. But what if he had decided to call this play by some other title, perhaps referring to a theme of the play? Suggest a few possible alternative titles that may have gone through his mind.

2 A man's world

The England of Queen Elizabeth I was very much a male world. The monarch was a woman, but power was predominantly in the hands of men. The world of *Henry IV Part 1* is even more obviously male. The three women who appear have little or no power to influence what happens. Because of this, the play has often been described as lacking in affection or sympathy.

Step into role as a committed feminist who has agreed to direct the play. Suggest some major features of your production. You might begin by considering whether the play appeals differently to males or females, and whether women have a different idea of 'honour' from men.

3 Ten points about Falstaff

You have been asked to talk to a group of school students about Falstaff. The teacher has suggested that you call your talk 'Ten things to remember about Falstaff'. Prepare and deliver your talk.

4 Hal – a changed man?

Many people argue that the play's major theme is the education of Prince Hal, and that Hal is the main character (see page 188).

Hal first appears in the world of the tavern. His father the king despairs of him, seeing him as wild and dissolute. By the end of the play, Hal, successful in battle, is accepted by his father as a noble prince.

Consider each scene in which Hal appears. Make notes to show how you would present him (costume, demeanour, and so on) in each scene. Also suggest the feelings towards Hal you would wish the audience to experience at different points in your own production of the play.

5 Dramatic construction

Shakespeare structures the play to ensure that each scene contrasts with its neighbouring scenes. Turn to the beginning of each scene and suggest how it comments in some way on the preceding scene, deepening meaning and dramatic effect. Consider characters, action, themes, and so on. You can find help on pages 10, 38 and 150.

6 Design opportunities

Choose one or more of these design tasks: a coat of arms for Falstaff; costumes for several characters; campaign medals for the battle of Shrewsbury; a poster advertising the play (study the cover of this edition and suggest which aspects of the play it symbolises).

7 Viewpoints

Work in a group of three. One of you is a confirmed royalist, one is a committed republican, the third holds no strong views either way. Argue your case for a production expressing your political belief.

8 Falstaff's recruits speak about honour

Only a few of Falstaff's recruits survive the battle of Shrewsbury. Step into role as a survivor and tell what honour means to you.

9 Fathers and son

The serious and comic plots contrast two types of father. Henry IV is a repressive, distant father, racked by his conscience for his sin in usurping the throne. Falstaff seems a warm and caring foster father. He is a role model of irresponsibility, excess and self-indulgence.

Hal must choose which father's values to adopt. Write two of his personal diary entries at the start and end of the play in which he declares his feelings for Falstaff and Henry.

10 An illustrated map

Copy the map on page 2. Illustrate each place name to signify what happens there: for example, quotations, coats of arms, and so on.

11 Television documentary

You have been commissioned to make a 30-minute documentary film about the Battle of Shrewsbury and the events that led up to it. Write your script. If you have a video camera, shoot your film.

What is the play about?

One way of thinking about *Henry IV Part 1* is to see it as Shakespeare's version of the morality plays which were very popular in medieval England. These plays portrayed the struggles between such characters as Vice and Virtue, in which Vice used all kinds of tricks to tempt a young man into disorderly behaviour and wrongdoing. But Virtue finally triumphed, and the young man was redeemed to goodness. Falstaff is obviously the tempter, and Hal calls him by the names of some of the characters of the old plays: 'Vice', 'Iniquity', 'Vanity'.

Another way of answering the question is to tell the story, for example by reading the summaries of the action at the top of each left-hand page. You might even try to tell the story in a single sentence: 'This history play shows how the unsuccessful rebellion by the Percy family against King Henry is mirrored by the comic subplot in which Prince Hal resists Falstaff's attempts to lead him astray.'

The play portrays Shakespeare's dramatic version of one year in the reign of King Henry IV. The Falstaff subplot reflects the main plot of political rebellion, and ironically comments upon and subverts it. From this viewpoint, the play can be seen as a satire on the morality of politics and war. The relationships of the two plots can be understood by considering some of the major themes of the play.

Honour

The word 'honour' rings through the play, and is much associated with the male characters. It was at the centre of the feudal tradition of chivalry, and involved bravery, duty and the conduct of a true knight. King Henry thinks Prince Hal has lost all honour by associating with Falstaff. Hotspur wants honour all for himself ('without corrival'), and thinks of it as gaining a reputation for bravery in military action.

Falstaff hopes that his lie that he killed Hotspur will bring him honour in the form of titles and wealth. His sardonic soliloquy on honour in Act 5 Scene 1 stands in striking contrast to Hotspur's ideal. Shakespeare's dramatic construction provides further ironic contrasts. Falstaff's soliloquy is immediately followed by Worcester's dishonourable decision to lie to Hotspur about King Henry's offer of peace.

Order and disorder

The very first words of the play introduce the theme of disorder:

'So shaken as we are, so wan with care'

King Henry is sick in body and troubled in mind. His disturbed conscience will not let him forget how he seized King Richard II's throne. He faces attacks from the Welsh and the Scots, and his former allies, the powerful Percy family who rule the North of England, threaten rebellion against him. He is grieved by his son, Prince Hal, and believes him abandoned to riot and disorder.

Many people believe that in his history plays, Shakespeare was dramatising 'the Tudor Myth'. This was a view of history that claimed that Henry Bullingbrook's deposition of King Richard II was an offence against God. God's punishment was almost a century of disorder until the first Tudor king, Henry VII, defeated Richard III at the battle of Bosworth in 1485 and restored order to England.

The argument goes that Elizabethans believed in 'the Great Chain of Being': a natural order in nature and society. According to this view (sometimes called 'the Elizabethan World Picture'), God sat at the top of a hierarchy, with angels below him, men and women below them and so on down to the smallest creatures and to inanimate matter.

This hierarchical model was applied in every sphere of life: the lion was the king of beasts, the rose the highest example of beauty, the king at the top of society. In families, the father was supreme, and men were superior to women. Such a hierarchical view was especially attractive to monarchs because they could claim that any rebellion against the king was a rebellion against God.

Not everyone in Shakespeare's time believed in this rigidly ordered system, but it was the official ideology of the ruling class, and it served their own interests very well. In churches, schools, history books and official proclamations, the message was preached that the existing hierarchical order was good, and that disorder was bad.

Shakespeare deepens the theme of disorder in the comic subplot. Just as Hotspur threatens political chaos, so Falstaff and his tavern colleagues represent the overthrow of authority as they lie, steal and seek personal advantage. They challenge and subvert hierarchy. The scene of the carriers in the inn yard at Rochester (Act 2 Scene 1) is emblematic of the theme: the old order has broken down, no man trusts another. Gadshill's talk of his accomplices shows that everyone in the land, from the highest to the lowest, is a highwayman of some kind.

Appearance and reality

As in every Shakespeare play, things are never what they seem. Prince Hal only pretends to be wild and riotous. For most of the play, all the other characters do not perceive his real intentions, but think he really is a madcap. Many kinds of deceptions occur. Henry IV has the appearance of a king, but he knows that in reality his title is weak. He puts many 'counterfeits' in the battlefield at Shrewsbury: knights dressed in his armour, pretending to be the king.

Falstaff claims to be a brave soldier and nobleman, and pretends to be dead on the battlefield of Shrewsbury. He may be a great liar, but his final soliloquy devastatingly reveals the grim reality that lies behind the appearance of 'honour'. The political plot also shows clearly that the talk of honour obscures the power-seeking that lies behind it, as the king and the feudal warlords struggle for domination.

The education of a Prince

The play has been interpreted as Hal's search for identity as, from his association with Falstaff and the other tavern characters, he learns about the ordinary people of England. This interpretation claims that Hal gains the common touch and becomes fit to rule as he jokes and plays among his low-life companions. It argues that the play is about 'growing up': the development of Hal's character as he makes his choice between idleness and the hard work of royal duty, between the tavern and the court. Hal recovers the reputation he has lost, and turns from irresponsible madcap to a powerful military and political leader.

Hal is compared to the Prodigal Son in the Bible (see page 190). His waste of time in foolery and horseplay in the tavern is seen as a rite of passage, the ritual through which he is transformed from adolescent to adult. He changes from someone who merely plays at being a prince to a true prince, fit to rule eventually as King Henry V.

England

Shakespeare's portrayal of England in the play takes many different forms. The frequently occurring place names give England a physical presence: Holmedon, Gad's Hill, Severn, Coventry, Shrewsbury, and other locations. So too do such mentions of 'boroughs, cities, villages', 'market crosses' and so on.

By constructing his play into alternating scenes of Court, Tavern and Rebels, Shakespeare conveys a complex social and symbolic picture of England. That picture is far from the stereotype of 'Merrie England'.

Although King Henry desperately wishes to unify his land, his first speech imagines England as a mother drinking her own children's blood. The sickness of the king mirrors the sickness of the country.

The rebels wish to carve up England between them. Their rebellion is a struggle for the material wealth of England. In the same way, the tavern subplot can be seen as a struggle for England's spiritual health, with Falstaff trying to gain control over Prince Hal, winning him to anarchy and self-interest.

The Falstaff scenes greatly extend the play's vision of England as they suggest the sheer variety of everyday life: eating, drinking, play-acting, popular mythology, ballads and brothels, religion and army life. Falstaff's frequent use of proverbs, biblical quotations and everyday knowledge conveys a vigorous sense of Shakespeare's own Elizabethan England.

But the presentation of England is far from complete. Women play little part in the drama. Hal's mother never appears; he has no lover. Kate, for all her liveliness, must submit to Hotspur's impetuous nature. Lady Mortimer's language cuts her off from her husband. Similarly, the working class play only minor or 'absent' parts, pressed into service to help the king and the nobles divide up the 'commonwealth' between them.

Activities on themes

a Turn to the list of characters on page 3 and place each character in order, with those 'most concerned with honour' at the top of your list, and those 'least concerned with honour' at the bottom.

b In one stage production, a model of an avenging angel hung over each of the court scenes. It illustrated the theme of God's punishment of Henry in bringing disorder to England by his seizure of the throne. Design a stage prop to use as a constant reminder of some major theme of the play.

c Write your own story of the play, first in a single sentence, next in a paragraph of five or six sentences. Then work in a group and dramatise your own two-minute version of the play.

d Other themes include: fathers and sons; debts and obligations (every character 'owes' something to other characters); friendship (are the friendships in the play real or pretended?). Identify characters, incidents and lines to suggest how each theme occurs in the play.

Characters

Prince Hal– 'the nimble-footed madcap Prince of Wales'

The Prince of Wales is often compared to the Prodigal Son in the Bible (Luke 15.11–32), who lived a life of self-indulgence and pleasure. He eventually repented and was forgiven by his father, who restored all his wealth and possessions. Like the Prodigal Son, Hal also turns over a new leaf, and wins his father's forgiveness.

Prince Hal must discover his destiny among people who represent very different values. He moves between three worlds as the pictures opposite show. Each presents him with choices he must make to help him succeed in his future role as King Henry V:

The Tavern – Falstaff's world: Here, Hal acts the playboy, sowing his wild oats, encouraged in his wildness and irresponsibility by his substitute father, Falstaff. In this society he gains knowledge of his future subjects and of himself.

The Court – King Henry's world: A stern, formal world of duty. It is ruled by a cold father who has no trust in his son, thinking him interested only in 'barren pleasures, rude society'.

The Battlefield – Hotspur's world: Here, Hal is contrasted with Hotspur, the model of chivalry and bravery, who seeks honour and glory, and dismisses Hal as a 'nimble-footed madcap'.

All three worlds mistakenly view Hal as wild and dissolute, living only for pleasure. But Hal's soliloquy at the end of Act 1 Scene 2 reveals that he is merely pretending. He intends to play the madcap role only for as long as it suits his purpose. When the time comes, he will abandon his riotous ways. He will thus redeem himself to glittering effect, so that his reformation will seem even more praiseworthy in the eyes of his subjects.

Hal's soliloquy has been differently interpreted as a major clue to his character. One view sees him as cold and calculating, heartless and manipulative as he unscrupulously uses other people to achieve his own ends. He is very much a chip off the old block, the image of his cold-blooded father.

A more favourable interpretation is that he is shrewd and pragmatic. He genuinely enjoys the excitement, warmth and friendship he finds in the tavern, and it satisfies a playful streak in his nature. But his tavern experience is an exercise in statecraft, helping him find his true vocation as king. At Shrewsbury he displays his courage and chivalry, together with his generosity as he pardons the captured Douglas.

Write a set of notes for the actor playing Hal to guide his performance, suggesting how you hope the audience feel about him at different moments in the play.

(right) The Court, a world of duty: Hal and his father, King Henry
(below) The Tavern, a world of licence: Hal with Falstaff

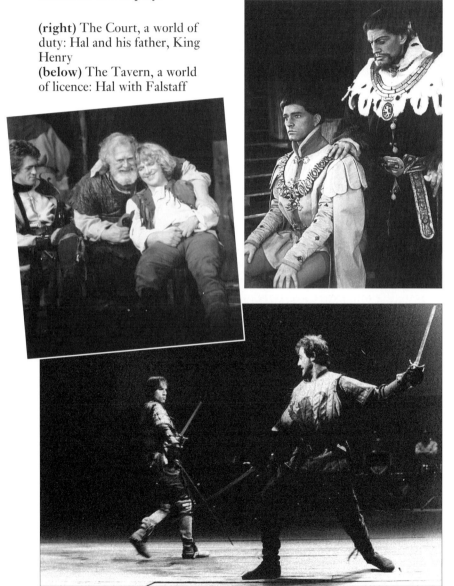

(above) The Battlefield, a world of action: Hal and Hotspur

Falstaff – 'That villainous abominable misleader of youth'

Ever since Falstaff first stepped on stage over four hundred years ago, he has enjoyed great success. Audiences took the fat knight to their hearts in spite of his very obvious faults.

Falstaff has been called a thief, liar, parasite, drunkard, lecher, braggart, swindler, toady (sycophant), fraud, sponger and coward. He is totally egocentric, dedicated to pleasure, and ruled by his appetite for food and drink, sleep and women. He exploits others for his own advantage, and is always concerned to save his own skin. Devoid of morality, he is self-seeking, unscrupulous and corrupt.

But for all his defects, Falstaff has been hugely popular. He lives on his wits and has great resourcefulness and presence of mind. He is a rugged individualist without malice or hypocrisy, and is a clear-sighted critic of the power-seeking and folly of his society. The sheer variety of differing views about Falstaff can be seen in the ways in which his dramatic function has been described:

Father: He is a substitute father for Hal, his warmth and friendship opposed to the cold and disapproving King Henry IV.

Educator: Falstaff helps Hal learn about a quite different world from the court – the ordinary people he will one day rule over as king.

Sceptic: As a kind of 'Holy Fool', Falstaff constantly challenges and subverts authority and traditional values, revealing their hypocrisy.

Vice: a cowardly, boastful character in medieval morality plays who tempted young men away from virtue (see page 186).

Miles gloriosus: a braggart, fraudulent, soldier in Italian comedies. He pretended to be brave, but was a rank coward.

Fool: a comic character, a buffoon or clown who revelled in witty wordplay. Fools often assumed a mock piety and morality, to expose the double standards of conventional society.

Lord of Misrule: In medieval festivals, a Lord of Misrule was appointed or elected for a short period. He was often portrayed as a grotesque figure with a giant appetite for food, drink, sex and riot. He presided over a spirit of carnival that challenged and defied conventional hierarchy and values, licensing all kinds of opposition to authority and responsibility. But, like Falstaff, his days were numbered.

Scapegoat: Falstaff will eventually be rejected and driven out, taking with him the stain and dishonour of Hal's riotous youth (see *Henry IV Part 2*).

In the first performances of the play, Falstaff was originally called Oldcastle. Oldcastle's descendants still held high office under Queen Elizabeth I, and they objected to seeing their famous ancestor scandalously misrepresented and made into a figure of fun on stage. Their protests led to Shakespeare changing the fat knight's name when the play was published in 1598.

The original Sir John Oldcastle was a famous Protestant hero and martyr. As a young man he had been a friend of Prince Hal, and he fought bravely in France for King Henry V. But Oldcastle became a Lollard, a member of a Protestant movement that vigorously challenged the dominant Catholic orthodoxy in England.

The Lollards were considered as heretics who blasphemed against the 'true' religion, and the punishment for heresy was death. For his beliefs, Oldcastle was burnt at the stake on Christmas Day 1417, aged only 39.

The American actor James Hackett (1800–71) played Falstaff wearing an enormous airbag underneath his costume to create a gigantic paunch. But one of his fellow actors disliked Hackett, and at one performance pricked a hole in the false stomach so that it slowly collapsed. Hackett gradually decreased in size until at last, with a rush of wind, the stomach disappeared altogether. Hackett finished the scene as best he could, but the audience was helpless with laughter.

King Henry – 'this vile politician'

King Henry has blood on his hands and a troubled conscience. He is weighed down by guilt, because he deposed King Richard II, and caused his murder. Henry proposes to lead a Crusade to the Holy Land to ease the burden of his conscience. He knows his title to the crown is weak, but wishes to leave a united kingdom and a secure, legitimate title to his eldest son, Prince Hal.

Both these desires seem to be frustrated. Henry's former allies have joined with the Welsh and Scots and are in rebellion against him. Hal's wild behaviour seems likely to cause England to collapse into chaos after he becomes King.

But for all King Henry's sickness in mind and body, he proves a skilful and decisive ruler. He is a man of action, arrogantly overriding opposition and shrewdly and ruthlessly directing the affairs of state. He moves swiftly to counter the rebels' challenge. He teaches a lesson in statecraft to Hal in Act 3 Scene 2, describing the contrast between the over-familiarity of King Richard and his own aloof behaviour ('ne'er seen but wondered at').

a Shakespeare portrays King Henry as old and ill, but in real life he was only 37 at the time of the battle of Shrewsbury. Henry probably suffered from leprosy and became increasingly worried about his appearance, unwilling to show himself in public. In the BBC production of the play, King Henry was shown in each scene compulsively wiping his hands with a cloth (the first signs of leprosy often appear on the hands). If you were playing the part, how would you portray him?

b What are Henry's feelings for Hal? Does he love him as a person, or is he just worried about ensuring the crown passes peacefully to Hal? Step into role as Henry and declare your feelings.

Hotspur – 'this gunpowder Percy'

Harry Percy's nickname, 'Hotspur', suggests his fiery temperament. He seems to have only one thing on his mind: 'honour'. For him that means glory and fame won in battle, even though it gives him troubled dreams. He wants honour for himself alone ('without corrival') and he despises caution and delay. He is Shakespeare's portrait of a man in single-minded pursuit of the idea of chivalry.

Such single-mindedness results in poor political judgement. For all his bravery as a soldier, Hotspur is a political failure. He is easily manipulated by his uncle Worcester, forgets the map at the rebels' conference, constantly mocks and provokes his ally Glendower, and underestimates both King Henry and Prince Hal. Rashly thinking he can overcome any obstacle, he fights at Shrewsbury against superior numbers. His uncle Worcester summarises his defects (Act 3 Scene 1, lines 177–9):

> '... harsh rage,
> Defect of manners, want of government,
> Pride, haughtiness, opinion, and disdain'

Make a 'quotation collage' to display aspects of Hotspur's character, by selecting two or three of his lines from each scene in which he appears.

Other characters

Use the following brief descriptions as the starting point for your investigation of a chosen character. Identify each scene in which your character appears and suggest their motives for acting and speaking as they do, together with how you think other characters view them.

Worcester – A self-seeking, shrewd politician, who cynically and easily manipulates Hotspur. Does he really care for Mortimer, or just for the Percy family?

Poins – More intelligent than Prince Hal? Is he high or low social class? Why does he disappear after Act 2?

Kate – No wilting flower. She is the equal of her husband Hotspur, but always seems to lose out to him.

Hostess – Good-hearted, and much put upon by Falstaff who makes her the butt of his jokes.

Northumberland – Cautious and rational. He fails to arrive at Shrewsbury to support his son and the other rebels – why?

Glendower – Vain, boastful, full of supernatural imaginings. But he is also well-educated in poetry and music.

Douglas – Brave, blustering, a symbol of courage. There is much talk of his courage and chivalry, but he gets beaten in battle and runs away at Shrewsbury.

Mortimer– A peacemaker? Frustrated by his inability to speak his wife's language.

A number of low-status characters appear (Carriers, Francis and other barmen, messengers, Gadshill). Choose one character and tell the story of the play from their point of view.

The language of the play

Verse and prose

How did Shakespeare decide whether his characters should speak in verse or prose? A rough answer is that he followed the stage conventions of his time. His theatre audiences generally expected to hear high-status characters using verse, and prose used for comedy or by low-status characters.

Verse has the formal, ceremonious rhythm felt to be particularly suitable for the 'noble', 'serious' thoughts of kings and for great affairs of war and state. So whilst the 'comic' Falstaff scenes are in prose, the court and rebel scenes (with high-status characters) are mainly in blank verse (unrhymed verse). Each ten-syllable line of blank verse has five alternating unstressed (x) and stressed (/) syllables (iambic pentameter), as in the first line of the play:

```
x   /  x  /  x  /  x  /   x   /
So shaken as we are, so wan with care
```

Shakespeare uses verse or prose appropriate to the situation, 'serious' or 'comic'. Prince Hal has very high status, but he uses prose in the company of Falstaff and others of the tavern set ('comic'). But as the first tavern scene ends and he is left alone on stage, he switches to verse to declare his 'serious' intention to reject his low-status companions after they have served his purpose:

'I know you all, and will a while uphold
The unyoked humour of your idleness.'

a To experience the rhythm of iambic pentameter, read a few lines aloud from any of the verse speeches in the play. Pronounce each syllable very clearly, almost as if each were a separate word. As you speak, beat out the five-stress rhythm (clap your hands, or tap your desk).

b Trace Prince Hal's progress through the play, identifying when and where he uses verse and when and where prose. Suggest one or two reasons for why Shakespeare gives him verse or prose at each point.

c Invent a few blank verse lines describing your response to the play.

Imagery

Imagery is the use of vivid words and phrases that conjure up emotionally charged pictures in the imagination. When Falstaff tells Hal to rob the king's exchequer 'and do it with unwashed hands', the image of not pausing even to wash one's hands suggests that Hal should carry out the robbery instantly. Falstaff's description of his wretched soldiers as 'food for powder' is chillingly callous in its dismissal of men as merely the prey of gunpowder.

As the play begins, King Henry's image of England as a mother, drinking her children's blood, describes the horror of civil war in which Englishman fought Englishman:

'... the thirsty entrance of this soil
Shall daub her lips with her own children's blood'

Throughout the play Shakespeare uses imagery as a kind of verbal scene painting. Every page of the script contains examples of imagery. Major sources for images are: the natural world (animals, the sun as a monarch, the moon, and so on); the social world (commerce, thievery, scripture, and so on); the human body (head, hands, feelings, and so on).

Hotspur describes the posturing lord who so enraged him as a 'popinjay' (parrot); he calls King Henry a 'fawning greyhound'. Hal claims that when he reforms, his change will be 'like bright metal on a sullen ground'. King Henry says 'like a comet I was wondered at'. Falstaff employs a huge range of extravagant images in each scene in which he appears.

All Shakespeare's imagery uses metaphor or simile. Both are comparisons: a simile uses 'like' or 'as' in the comparison, a metaphor does not. When in his first speech King Henry speaks of 'frighted peace' and 'trenching war', he uses metaphors to describe the harshness of civil war. But when he pictures the two sides in the civil war as 'like the meteors of a troubled heaven' he uses a simile.

Personification is a particular type of imagery. It turns things or ideas into human beings, giving them human feelings or body parts. When Hotspur describes how Mortimer fought with Glendower, he speaks of the River Severn as 'gentle' and as being 'so affrighted' that it 'Ran fearfully' and 'hid his crisp head'.

Open any page of the script at random and identify as many images as you can. Find a way of enacting or displaying some of those images (for example, as an illustration or tableau).

Lists

One of Shakespeare's favourite methods with language was to accumulate words or phrases rather like a list. Such lists often express a vital aspect of the play by intensifying description, atmosphere or argument. Shakespeare knew that 'piling up' item on item, incident on incident, can increase dramatic effect, whether serious or comic.

Some lists are long, for example, Hal's first speech, listing Falstaff's vices (Act 1 Scene 2, lines 2–9); Gadshill's catalogue of criminals (Act 2 Scene 1, lines 59–64); Lady Percy's description of a dozen elements of Hotspur's disturbed dreams (Act 2 Scene 3, lines 44–9). Other lists are short but just as revealing of character or theme, for example in Hotspur's joy at the prospect of war (Act 1 Scene 3, line 296):

'Till fields, and blows, and groans applaud our sport!'

Lists of all types and purposes occur. They can be descriptions of persons (Hotspur's tale of the popinjay lord who so enraged him at Holmedon, or King Henry's description of King Richard II). They can describe an event or past sequence of history (the fight between Mortimer and Glendower, or the story of Henry's seizing of the throne as told by Hotspur in Act 4 Scene 3 and Worcester in Act 5 Scene 1). Lists can also be like the development of a reasoned argument (Falstaff's soliloquy on honour). Or, like the many insults that Falstaff and Hal exchange, lists use humour to reveal character.

a Turn at random to three or four pages of the script. On every page you will find a list of some kind. Suggest what kind of list it is, and what function it fulfils in the play. Speak each list in a style you think suitable. Try to give each item in the list its own special emphasis or tone, to make it distinctive and memorable. Some of your lists will lend themselves to acting out.

b Experiment with changing the order of words in some lists. Suggest why you think Shakespeare decided that the order he chose was the most dramatically powerful.

Language is character

Shakespeare gives each character a distinctive language, suitable to the speaker's meaning and mood. Hotspur uses a warlike, military vocabulary. His fiery words tumble out impetuously, often in short phrases and vivid imagery. Glendower's language is often mystical and poetic. Vernon speaks the lyrical language of chivalry to describe Hal.

The two Carriers speak in their own distinctive style, their language filled with the concrete realities of the hard life of the medieval working class. Gadshill and the Chamberlain talk in a kind of thieves' slang.

Every character uses language appropriate to their situation. Prince Hal switches from prose to verse as he moves from the tavern to the court. King Henry may begin wearily, but his tone becomes businesslike and angry with the rebels.

Falstaff's language is dazzlingly various and inventive, intensely physical. He lies, boasts, insults, puns, ridicules, blusters and talks nonsense, all with an exuberant imaginative energy. Never at a loss for an answer, words are his way of getting out of trouble as he talks himself out of tight spots. However overblown or fantastic his imagery, it usually contains a telling truth or critical judgement. Three characteristics of his language are:

Gigantic exaggeration: He monstrously inflates the number of his attackers at Gad's Hill, and piles insult on insult, image on image, lie on lie, in riotous accumulation.

Mock piety: He pretends to be virtuous and religious, using biblical quotations and Puritan sayings. He puts on an air of outraged dignity, amazed at the evils of the world ('Lord, how this world is given to lying').

Irony: He uses parody and satire to mock authority and conventional values. He mimics others (Hal, King Henry, Hotspur) and constantly uses humour to undermine and subvert hierarchy and traditional values, most notably in his questioning of 'honour'.

a Hal and Falstaff insult each other in memorable phrases in Act 2 Scene 4: 'thou clay-brained guts', 'you bull's-pizzle', and so on. Collect up each insult, take parts, and exchange your insults, accompanying each with an appropriate gesture.

b In this edition, Hotspur and his allies are called 'rebels', and their fight against King Henry is described as 'rebellion'. But you don't have to accept that 'rebel' is the most appropriate description of Hotspur. As history teaches, today's 'rebel' is tomorrow's 'freedom fighter'. The description of any character depends on the point of view of the speaker and the power he or she has to make any label stick. Turn to the list of characters on page 3 and rewrite it from Hotspur's point of view.

History into drama

In *Henry IV Part 1*, Shakespeare dramatises a year in King Henry's reign from 22 June 1402, when Mortimer was captured by the Welsh, to 21 July 1403, the battle of Shrewsbury. Shakespeare's dramatic imagination was fired by all kinds of things he had heard, seen or read. For example, like other Elizabethans, he probably enjoyed the many folk tales and legends that were told about the supposed wildness of Prince Hal before he became king.

As someone passionately interested in theatre, Shakespeare probably saw some of the very popular chronicle plays that presented patriotic scenes from English history. One of them, *The Famous Victories of Henry the Fifth*, much performed in the 1590s, presented Prince Hal as a wild young man who robbed, drank and play-acted in the company of Jockey Oldcastle (Falstaff) and Ned (Poins).

Shakespeare may also have been influenced by accounts of medieval morality plays (see page 186) which presented a young man tempted into mischief by Vice, but redeemed by Virtue. The alternation of scenes of comedy and seriousness in such plays is reflected in Shakespeare's dramatic construction of *Henry IV*.

As he wrote *Henry IV*, Shakespeare used his reading to help him mould history into dramatic form. His major source was Holinshed's *Chronicles of England, Scotland and Ireland*. First published in 1577, the second edition of 1587 was at his side as he wrote the play. A number of Shakespeare's scenes follow Holinshed quite closely, and he includes the same mistakes as Holinshed, for example in confusing two Edmund Mortimers.

Holinshed presented history from the standpoint of the Tudor dynasty that ruled Shakespeare's England. He portrayed Henry IV's overthrow of Richard II as the sinful act that brought down God's punishment on England in the horrors of civil war throughout most of the fifteenth century (see page 187).

In his history plays, Shakespeare dramatises the political, social and personal preoccupations of his own time. For example, a question that lies at the heart of the play ('Who is the rightful monarch?') reflects the contemporary anxiety concerned with who should succeed Queen Elizabeth I. Elizabethans also probably saw a political lesson in the play on the evils of rebellion. To many in Shakespeare's audience, believing in national unity, the sight of Hotspur and his fellow rebels dividing the country into three parts was proof of the unlawfulness of the Percies' rebellion.

Elizabethans were fervently interested in history and issues of national identity. They saw the troubled fifteenth century rather as Americans look back on their own Civil War: distant in time, but still intensely relevant.

Shakespeare's contemporaries were fascinated by power politics and felt that history could provide instruction and guidance. They saw a moral lesson in the spectacle of a future king pretending to be wild and abandoned, but all the time planning to throw off his loose behaviour and companions in order to rule wisely and well.

Although Shakespeare followed his historical sources fairly closely, he altered and added to suit his dramatic purposes, to create conflict and to balance characters. For example, Hotspur was in fact three years older than King Henry, but to heighten the Hal–Hotspur conflict, Shakespeare makes him the same age as Hal and makes King Henry appear older than he actually was (see page 152).

Shakespeare compressed or rearranged certain historical events to heighten dramatic effect. He makes Hotspur's victory at Holmedon occur at the same time as Mortimer's defeat by Glendower (it actually took place three months later). He shifts Henry's desire to go on a Crusade from the end to the beginning of his reign. He invents Hal's rescue of King Henry at Shrewsbury, and gives Prince John an heroic part in the battle (at which the thirteen-year-old John did not fight).

The comic plot shows Shakespeare at his most inventive. He creates Falstaff and his tavern companions as an ironic parallel and contrast to the political plot, notably as Falstaff conducts his own 'rebellion' and questions the value of 'honour'. For example, in Act 1, Henry's plan for a military campaign is followed by Falstaff's plan for a robbery.

a Imagine someone says to you 'I'm worried about Shakespeare because he so often presents a false view of history. Look at all the alterations and mistakes he makes about what really happened in the reign of King Henry IV'. What do you reply?

b A wealthy sponsor is willing to give you funds to put on a production if you can give her seven reasons why *Henry IV Part 1* is relevant to young people today. Convince her!

Staging the play

Henry IV Part 1 was probably written around 1596–7. It was a success from the moment it was first performed. During Shakespeare's life, it was printed more frequently than any other of his plays. First published in 1598, a total of six editions of the play were published (Quartos) before it appeared in the First Folio of 1623.

Falstaff proved so popular that Shakespeare wrote two further plays about the fat knight: *Henry IV Part 2* and *The Merry Wives of Windsor*. Adaptations long after Shakespeare's death exploited Falstaff's appeal in plays with such names as *The Bouncing Knight*, or *The Robbers Robbed*, and *The Boaster or Bully-Huff catched in a Trap*.

In eighteenth- and nineteenth-century England, many famous actors played Falstaff. In America the play was equally popular. The nineteenth century saw spectacular productions trying to create the world of medieval England on stage. Their large casts, elaborate costumes, sets and props were a great contrast to the open bare stage of Shakespeare's Elizabethan theatre.

For three hundred years, Falstaff was the main attraction of the play, but the twentieth century has seen major changes in staging:

- emphasis on the power politics of the play, with the Falstaff scenes paralleling and ironically commenting on the serious plot.
- highlighting of the father–son relationships in the play, particularly between Hal and his real father, King Henry, and substitute father, Falstaff.
- presentation as part of a cycle of history plays to show the progress of the Lancastrian dynasty that Henry IV founded (see opposite). Sometimes *Part 1* is paired with *Part 2* (which shows the rejection of Falstaff). Sometimes Henry V is added to the cycle, to show Hal as King, triumphing at Agincourt. Other cycles begin with *Richard II* to show how Henry Bullingbrook seized the throne. Both the Royal Shakespeare Company and the English Shakespeare Company have presented the full cycle of eight history plays (with heavy adaptation of the three Henry VI plays) to show all of Shakespeare's story of the working out of the consequences of Henry's unlawful overthrow of King Richard II.

The cycle of Shakespeare's history plays

Richard II tells how Henry Bullingbrook deposes King Richard and is crowned as King Henry IV.

Henry IV Parts 1 and *2* tell of Prince Hal's exploits with Falstaff, his victory at Shrewsbury over Hotspur (*Part 1*), and how he finally rejects Falstaff when he becomes king (*Part 2*).

Henry V tells of Henry's victory at Agincourt and his betrothal to Katherine, the French King's daughter.

Henry VI Parts 1, *2* and *3* tell how Henry VI loses the English possessions in France and sees his kingdom racked by civil war (the Wars of the Roses). Henry is murdered by the Duke of Gloucester who later becomes King Richard III.

Richard III tells how Richard murders his way to the English throne, but is eventually overthrown by Richmond who becomes Henry VII, so establishing the Tudor dynasty.

The play has traditionally been performed in Elizabethan or medieval costumes and settings. Some recent productions have used modern dress and settings, for example with tavern characters as football hooligans. The picture shows a French production set in the Japan of the samurai period. Hal, left, saves his father (lying down) from Douglas. The red ribbons streaming from Douglas' mouth are used in Japanese theatre to signify blood.

William Shakespeare 1564–1616

1564 Born Stratford-upon-Avon, eldest son of John and Mary Shakespeare.
1582 Marries Anne Hathaway of Shottery, near Stratford.
1583 Daughter, Susanna, born.
1585 Twins, son and daughter, Hamnet and Judith, born.
1592 First mention of Shakespeare in London. Robert Greene, another playwright, described Shakespeare as 'an upstart crow beautified with our feathers …'. Greene seems to have been jealous of Shakespeare. He mocked Shakespeare's name, calling him 'the only Shake-scene in a country' (presumably because Shakespeare was writing successful plays).
1595 A shareholder in 'The Lord Chamberlain's Men', an acting company that became extremely popular.
1596 Son Hamnet dies, aged eleven.
     Father, John, granted arms (acknowledged as a gentleman).
1597 Buys New Place, the grandest house in Stratford.
1598 Acts in Ben Jonson's *Every Man in His Humour*.
1599 Globe Theatre opens on Bankside. Performances in the open air.
1601 Father, John, dies.
1603 James I grants Shakespeare's company a royal patent: 'The Lord Chamberlain's Men' became 'The King's Men' and played about twelve performances each year at court.
1607 Daughter, Susanna, marries Dr John Hall.
1608 Mother, Mary, dies.
1609 'The King's Men' begin performing indoors at Blackfriars Theatre.
1610 Probably returned from London to live in Stratford.
1616 Daughter, Judith, marries Thomas Quiney.
     Dies. Buried in Holy Trinity Church, Stratford-upon-Avon.

The plays and poems
(no one knows exactly when he wrote each play)

1589–1595 *The Two Gentlemen of Verona, The Taming of the Shrew, First, Second and Third Parts of King Henry VI, Titus Andronicus, King Richard III, The Comedy of Errors, Love's Labour's Lost, A Midsummer Night's Dream, Romeo and Juliet, King Richard II* (and the long poems *Venus and Adonis* and *The Rape of Lucrece*).

1596–1599 *King John, The Merchant of Venice, First and Second Parts of King Henry IV, The Merry Wives of Windsor, Much Ado About Nothing, King Henry V, Julius Caesar* (and probably the *Sonnets*).

1600–1605 *As You Like It, Hamlet, Twelfth Night, Troilus and Cressida, Measure for Measure, Othello, All's Well That Ends Well, Timon of Athens, King Lear.*

1606–1611 *Macbeth, Antony and Cleopatra, Pericles, Coriolanus, The Winter's Tale, Cymbeline, The Tempest.*

1613 *King Henry VIII, The Two Noble Kinsmen* (both probably with John Fletcher).

1623 Shakespeare's plays published as a collection (now called the First Folio).